# URBAN

# Forest School

# URBAN

# Forest School

## Outdoor Adventures and Skills for City Kids

Naomi Walmsley & Dan Westall

# Contents

What is urban forest school? 6
Climate change 14
Useful knots 16

## In the park or garden

Outdoor theatre 22
*Garden memories* 24
Easel tree 26
Biodegradable bird feeders 27
Honey bee water station 32
Snail race 33
Botanical interactive art 34
Giant bubbles 36
Bubble snake maker 38
Nature weaving 40
Outdoor games 42
Shadow painting 44
Fizzy mud pies 46
*A city camping adventure* 48
Willow hanging ball 50
Sheet dens 52
Nature's board games 56
Track traps 58

## Around the city or town

Cloud spotting 64
City wildlife spotter 66
City sit spot 70
*Grass snake* 72
Bug superpowers 74
Know your trees 76
Plant power 80
*Suburban surroundings* 84
Town and city scavenger hunt 86
Colour chart nature matching 88
A night walk 90

## Home crafts

Felted soap dinky 96
Eco leaf printing 98
Leaf watercolour printing 100
Pine-cone deer 103
Measuring stick 104
Beeswax wraps 106
Nature journal 108
Leaf bunting 112
Planting and using herbs 114
Berries in your boots 116
Sack of potatoes 117
Stick boats 118
Track shoes 120
Nest challenge 123
Felted nature bag 124
Natural seed balls 128
Things to do with conkers 130

## Recipes

A guide to foraging 134
Soothing salves 136
Stinging nettle crisps 138
Stinging nettle smoothie 139
Garlic and butter nettles 140
Barbecue bannock bread 142
Garlic mustard pesto sauce 143
Dandelion cookies 144
Dandelion honey 145
*Dinner at the allotment* 146
Blackberry chutney 148
Spiced blackberry sorbet 149
Blackberry and apple crumble 150

Track templates 154
Resources/About the authors 156
Acknowledgements 157
Index 158

# What is urban forest school?

*Forest school is all about connecting young children to their natural environment, creating opportunities to develop creativity, confidence, resilience and learning, as well as promoting ways in which children can experience risk. Therefore Urban Forest School is exactly the same, just with a few little creative tweaks, an extra dose of exploration, imagination and time taken to look around you.*

Being outdoors and immersed in nature isn't just for people who live in the countryside. When you live in a rural area, it is easy to immerse yourself in nature. It's obvious, it's right there in front of you, shouting loudly at you to come and play. It's easy to forget that even when you live in cities and towns, nature is right there, just waiting to be found and enjoyed by you.

You don't need a woodland to be able to hunt for bugs. You don't need a garden to make mud pies, you don't need a vast green space to play games and you don't need fields and meadows to look for plants and wildlife. You can create your own nature space or, even better, spend some time searching it out. You may be surprised by what you see around you.

As you start to look, making time to take in the world around you, you'll see spiders building webs on car wing mirrors, grass and weeds growing through cracks in pavements, trees in their various seasonal splendour lining city streets, birds building nests in school playgrounds and plenty more. Nature truly surrounds us if we just open our eyes a little wider and know where to look.

# Using this book

This book is both instructional and informative, teaching children (and adults) about their world, the trees, the bugs, beasties and creatures within it and how to find, explore, use and understand it. There are activities for all ages, from creative messy mud play for curious pre-schoolers to medicinal salve making and willow weaving for the more advanced age groups. You can dip into this book, using it in different ways: to identify plants, learn about the planet, its wildlife and its stars, read a story, learn how to make crafts or inspire you to take a night walk.

Begin your journey through busy towns and concrete cities, cloud spotting, identifying plants, looking deep into grass-filled cracks, hunting for bugs and foraging. Open up your imagination through step-by-step guides to crafting at home and find new ways of exploring your local park and garden. All of these will encourage you to look at your towns and cities in a new light. There are recipes to transform 'weeds' into delicious treats and healing medicines and games to bring on the fun.

As well as activities, this book also offers information about how to look after the planet and reasons why we should all do this, giving both adults and children a new and fresh perspective on the word 'nature'. There's even a section on climate change to help inspire everyone to take care of their outdoor environment. Intertwined throughout this book are moving and entertaining anecdotes collected from people who have special memories of interacting with or discovering nature in unexpected or urban environments, bringing this book alive with stories.

# Where can I look for urban nature?

## Look up

Observe the clouds, the birds, bees and butterflies. See the sunshine through the leaves in the trees; try catching rain on your tongue. What about looking up at night time? Study the waxing and waning of the moon's cycles. Can you see any stars?

## Look down

Bugs don't just roam in gardens, they like to hide in pavements too. Find sticks and leaves on the ground to make into crafts or transform into a wand, a sword or a stick buddy just by using your imagination.

## Parks

Parks are great for their playgrounds, but what's in the surrounding area? Is there a tree to safely climb, a stream to explore, a wooded area, an area of flowers to smell, touch, fill your eyes with colour?

## Allotments

Many of us don't have a garden or outdoor area but maybe you could get yourself on a waiting list for an allotment or community garden. Growing up, our family allotment was one of my favourite places to spend time, helping to prepare the soil, tending and watching the vegetables grow and, finally, enjoying eating them. Although my favourite activity was raspberry stealing from my mother's prize patch while pretending to help pick beans!

## Cemeteries

Who would have thought that a cemetery could be so full of life? Often, the most amazing wildflowers bloom, delicious blackberries grow undiscovered, hundred-year-old yew trees grow, their roots spreading overground. Stick to the paths though and be respectful of where you roam, as well as respectful to other people in these areas. They may be here to visit a loved one and hoping for a quiet moment.

## Why is playing outside good for us?

There have been numerous studies on why we feel better outdoors. It's due to the fact that we're active and moving around and that we can feel the elements and breathe a little freer. We use our imaginations more when we are outside, we use our bodies and we use our hands. Playing outdoors encourages resilience, self-confidence, initiative and creativity to grow. It highlights the joy of movement, nurtures wild imaginations, experimentation, friendships and social connections, and helps develop positive behaviours.

When our outdoor experience includes nature play, we feel even better. We can see life around us, weaving webs, flying in the sky,

## Are there any dangers?

There are always some risks, but without them I believe that we do not learn. It is not about removing these risks but how we manage them that makes the difference and keeps us safe from harm.

In an urban setting especially, like wastelands or urban parks, there is a greater risk of coming across things like needles and broken glass. Rubbish can be a big issue in built-up areas and can leave them not only untidy looking but occasionally can be quite dangerous, if touched. Even if you feel like you want to tidy up, it's advisable not to touch anything. Contact your local council if you feel like it's a big issue or come back with thick gloves and a long-armed litter picker. Talk to children about the things they might see that they shouldn't touch and explain why they might pose a danger.

### Road safety

Walking is by far healthier than going by car, so try to explore by foot if you can. By knowing the rules of the road you can make sure you stay safe while out and about. Follow these simple guidelines:

• Always walk on the pavement or path if there is one – never stray on to the road.
• If there's no pavement, walk in single file on the right side of the road facing the traffic.
• When you need to cross the road, find a safe place to do so.
• Keep looking and listening for traffic before and while crossing.

### What to do if you get lost

Don't go out on your own and when out with others stay together. Of course there is always a small chance you might find yourself separated from your group and get lost. To help make sure this doesn't happen, have a plan in place, know your route and where you are heading and communicate with one another while out. If you are walking somewhere, walk in pairs so that you have a partner at all times. Have a well-known, safe spot to go to (away from the main road) and wait there if you find yourself lost. Then you'll know where to go and your friends and family will be able to find you.

### Respect your urban environment
• Leave only footprints
• Take only photographs
• Take your time
• Leave no trace

flowing, rustling and moving. It makes us feel good to be a part of it. When I hear the word nature it conjures up images of mountains, wildlife, meadows, forests, waterfalls and lush green trees. Maybe it does for you too. But nature isn't all about the grand picture. Nature play can be any activity that gets children active or thinking actively outdoors.

When we interact with nature, when we notice it, play with or in it, we take a moment to reconnect ourselves to our own roots. It's so easy to spend time on a computer or watching television and yes, probably fun too, but there are so many opportunities outside to feel energized, creative and peaceful.

I love the simplicity, the ease of what being outdoors offers for children. Knowing where the best mud is to make mud pies, foraging for wild strawberries, making bug houses, finding ladybirds, drawing with chalk, making potions and perfume out of petals: the list is endless.

Every time we go outside, we are learning to cherish nature, to respect it, to pay attention to it and learn from it. It is during these moments that we grow, develop and learn as well as feeling happier and more content, so why not go looking for it?

## Embracing the weather

Fair weather playing is easy; the sun is out
and it automatically feels good to be outside.
It's getting out in the wind and the rain where
the adventures often can be found. In the
rain, there are massive puddles for stomping
through and opportunities for bug watching,
seeing the slithering and interesting bugs that
come out to hydrate. The rain makes great
mud for building, sculpting and playing in.
Or what about the wind? Simply just putting
your arms out and flying in the wind, flying a
kite on a hill or a leaf-kicking windy walk will
make you feel blustery and alive.

I believe it's just as important to experience
all the seasons outside as it is to play in all
weathers, even if it's just for a short while! As
long as you are dressed appropriately, you will
have a great time.

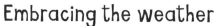

### Some simple ways to embrace the weather

**Make a kite** Get a paper bag with handles. Decorate it by sticking
on lots of leaves. Cut about 5yd (5m) of yarn or string. Find yourself
a straight-ish stick. Wrap one end of the yarn round and round the
stick and then the other end of the yarn on to the handles of your kite,
bringing them both together. Now fly in the wind, unwinding and
letting it out as the wind demands!

**Experiment with rain painting** Find some thick card, crushed-up
chalk, powder paints, pencil sharpener shavings of watercolour pencils
or broken-up watercolour paints. Dot the crushed colours all over the
card and leave it out in the rain for the drops to perform an art attack!

# Nature kit

All the children and adults in our family love to go out on adventures. We love both major and micro adventures, from epic hikes up mountains to visiting a local park to hunt for giraffes, bears and spiders, whatever the favourite of the week may be. We have got it down to a fine art now; we grab a snack, a drink and the nature bag, which in theory is kept in the same place ready to go. Of course it always has the memories of the last trip sticking out of it, packed full of leaves bigger than our heads, interesting shaped or textured rocks, the occasional stick that played its part in a game and more than likely a pine cone or two as an obligatory item to collect when we're out and about.

My children also love to pack new random apparently 'essential' items in there. A wooden snake has made its way in, there's a mini teddy to hide and find and a book on ladybirds to refer to – these essential items change regularly. But we do have a core set of things in there that are always useful. In this book you'll find everything you need to make your own nature kit.

**A measuring stick** in case you need to refer to the size of something later in your reference books (see page 104).

**A journal** so that you can draw and record all your thoughts, drawings and interesting findings (see page 108).

**A felted bag** to keep it all in (see page 124).

**A pencil and some string** for tying up shelters and practising knots, and a pair of mini scissors to cut the string.

Of course you could pack it full of other useful things such as magnifying glasses, binoculars, identification books and more, but I like to travel light just with what I feel are my absolute essentials. Try it out though. Have an adventure. See what you need.

# Climate change

*You might think that climate change is something that just concerns adults – a bit complicated, a bit grown up, maybe even a bit boring? It really isn't that complicated, and I promise it's not boring at all. It's about your planet, the one we all live on together. We all love playing in nature and rely on it for our homes, our food and our fun! Almost every aspect of our lives is linked to it whether we realize it or not. We wouldn't be able to enjoy the activities in this book at all if we lost our trees and wildlife. So let's work together to protect our planet.*

## What exactly is climate change?

Climate change, or global warming, is the process of our planet heating up. Rising temperatures just mean nicer weather, right? Wrong! Unfortunately, the changing climate will cause our weather to become more extreme and unpredictable and, in some cases, dangerous. Some areas will get wetter, some will get hotter and lots of animals, as well as us humans, could find they're not able to adapt to their changing environment. Our planet has warmed by about 1.8°F (1°C) in the last 100 years. That doesn't sound like a lot, but it means big things for people and wildlife around the globe and the temperature is rising still.

## What is making these changes happen?

Humans are always discovering new ways to make our lives more comfortable and fun, and developing new ways to make things easier. We all take for granted the simplicity of turning on a light or boiling a kettle for hot water. We have invented and created incredible technologies like aeroplanes, cars, computers, smartphones, tablets, dishwashers, vacuum cleaners and many more. Most of us enjoy watching television, perhaps some of you play on computer games. The trouble is, all these

**Tip**
*Think of a sponsored activity you could do to raise money for an organization that protects endangered animals. Maybe you could do a night walk, or walk up your local hill twice in a row. Or both at the same time!*

things produce waste in one way or another and need energy to run them.

The energy to make and power all these modern appliances comes from burning fossil fuels like coal and oil, which releases huge amounts of carbon dioxide into the atmosphere, trapping heat and warming up the planet. At the same time, whole forests are being cut down all over the world, meaning that there are fewer trees globally to absorb the carbon dioxide in the air. As more and more carbon dioxide is produced as a result of human activity, the planet will continue to become warmer.

## How will it affect us?

People around the world may struggle to grow food. A lot of this food is what we buy in our supermarkets to eat.

When the Earth heats up, ice melts. It becomes water and goes into streams, rivers, lakes and seas. This means that our water levels are rising. This could cause floods and make it hard for people to live in the same places they have always lived.

Climate change can make it difficult for plants and animals to survive. For example, if the ice melts where polar bears live, they'll have nowhere to live and may become extinct.

### So what can I do?

Good question. Here are some simple ways in which YOU can make a change.

- Don't buy new toys/games. Why not organize a toy swap? Get your friends to bring round toys and games that they haven't played with in a while, or perhaps have grown out of, and swap them. You can always swap them back again later!

- Ask if you can walk to school. Or perhaps if it's too far away, could you walk a little of the way instead or maybe ride a bike?

- Turn off lights when you don't need them.

- Turn off computers and other devices when they are not being used.

- Reuse and recycle. Find ways to turn rubbish into something new, use it for crafts or help to sort it for recycling.

- Buy a reuseable water bottle that you can refill every day.

- Don't use plastic straws. You don't really need one anyway!

- Buy second-hand things. Pre-loved stuff is much cheaper and much less harmful then producing new stuff.

- Plant food to eat, even if it's just herbs (see page 114). Producing your own food is both helpful and really healthy.

- Talk to your friends about ways in which you can reduce your use of plastic and write down solutions in your nature journal (see page 108).

- Play outside as much as you can and switch off the devices inside.

*Tip*
*Find out if there are any tree-planting schemes near where you live that you and your friends and family could help out with. Remember, trees help clean our air by absorbing carbon dioxide in the atmosphere.*

The oceans will heat up. Warmer waters are killing coral reefs and sea life, so no more fish fingers for us!

Our food chain will be disrupted and much of our wildlife will struggle to survive.

## Climate change and Urban Forest School

When you are out and about in your town or city, notice any trees, plants, wildlife and nature that you can see and think about all that they do for us.

Think about the changing seasons. What would we normally expect to see at this time of year? What sort of weather and which types of wildlife? What changes can we actually see and are they different to what we would expect?

# Useful knots

*Knots are incredibly useful for lots of tasks, from tying your shoes to making sure your den doesn't fall down! They help develop hand-eye coordination skills and are great for a mind workout. The more you practise and put these knots to use, the more natural knot tying will become.*

## Clove hitch

The clove hitch is a fantastic knot for starting or finishing a lashing such as a shear lashing (see page 17).

### Step 1
Pass the working end of the rope around the pole.

### Step 2
Cross over the standing end.

### Step 3
Loop it back around the pole.

### Step 4
Thread it back under itself (a) and pull tight (b).

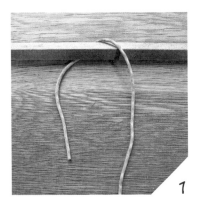

1

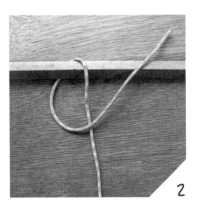

2

3

4a

4b

**Tip**
*Clove hitches work best on round poles.*

# Overhand knot

This is a really simple and useful knot to know. When pulled tight it can be used as a simple stopper knot.

### Step 1
Form a loop with the rope.

### Step 2
Pass the working end through the loop.

### Step 3
Tighten it to form the overhand knot.

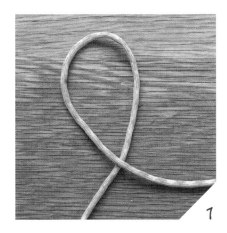

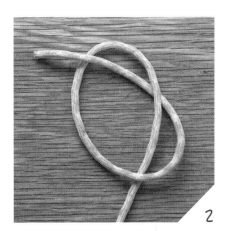

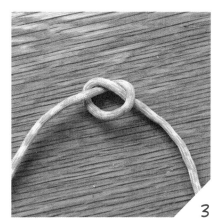

# Shear lashing

Use this simple knot to join two poles together.

### Step 1
Tie a clove hitch (see page 16) around one pole.

### Step 2
Wrap both poles with a simple lashing (weaving the working end in and out between the two poles), going round several times.

### Step 3
Wrap the lashings with three 'frapping turns' (wrapping them together three times, just simply round and round).

### Step 4
Tie off the end with another clove hitch.

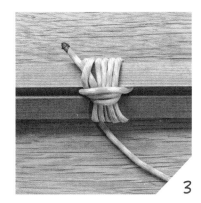

## Slip knot

This is a simple loop on the end of a string or rope that will loosen when the tail is pulled.

### Step 1

Form a loop at the end of your rope by placing the right-hand side of the rope on top of the left. Pinch the rope where it overlaps with your thumb and forefinger.

### Step 2

With your other hand, take the working end of the rope and push a loop through the back of the first loop you formed.

### Step 3

Pull until tight and the loop is secure. To release, pull the working end and the loop should slip through.

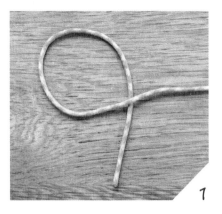

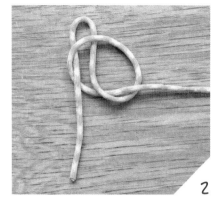

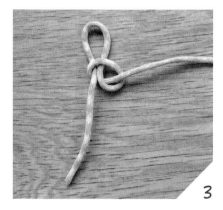

## Sheet bend

The sheet bend is a useful knot for tying two ropes together. You can even use two different types and thickness of ropes or string. This is a great knot when you find yourself needing that extra bit of length.

### Step 1

Form a loop in the end of one of the lengths of rope/string.

### Step 2

Pass the free end of the second rope that you want to be joined under the opening of the loop, around both parts of the first rope and back under itself.

### Step 3

Pull all four ends to tighten.

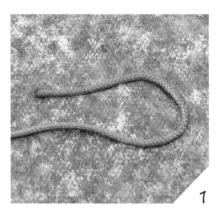

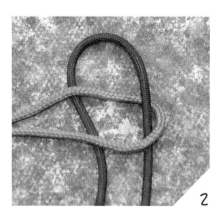

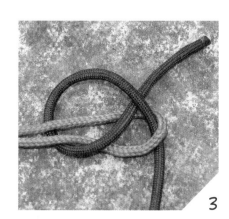

# Timber hitch

The timber hitch is a knot used to attach a single length of rope to a cylindrical object, like a tree. It is useful for pulling an object along as it locks when you apply pressure but unties easily when released.

### Step 1
Pass the rope around the log or tree.

### Step 2
Pass the rope over the standing end (the non-moving piece).

### Step 3
Bring the working end up on the log or tree.

### Step 4
Loop the working end around itself once.

### Step 5
Loop the working end around itself once more.

### Step 6
Then loop the working end around itself a third time. The friction of the knot will hold it tight and you can drag your load and secure the end to a tree to keep the tension while securing the other end.

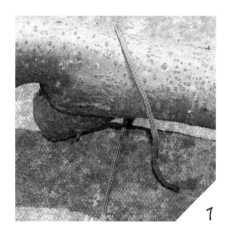

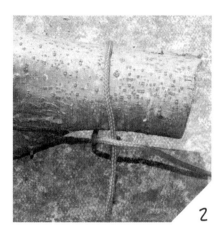

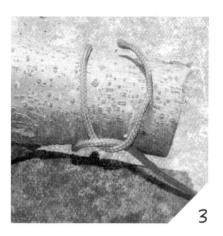

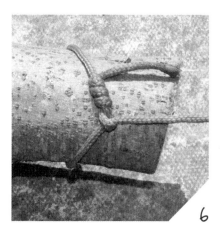

# In the park or garden

FOREST SCHOOL IS ALL ABOUT TRUSTING, UNDERSTANDING AND USING THE OUTDOOR ENVIRONMENT AND BUILDING A RELATIONSHIP WITH IT. THIS SECTION FOCUSES ON MAKING USE OF THE GREEN SPACES NEAR YOU. PERHAPS A GARDEN, MAYBE A PARK, OR SOMETIMES JUST HAVING ACCESS TO A SAFE, QUIET STREET OR FRONT PORCH WILL DO! HERE YOU CAN FOLLOW SIMPLE CRAFT PROJECTS, LEARN NEW GAMES AND CREATE AREAS WHERE YOUR IMAGINATION CAN RUN WILD.

# Outdoor theatre

*Children never seem to get bored of putting on shows and can be kept occupied for hours with puppet shows, singing contests, elaborate 'interpretive' dance recitals and full-on scripted shows, as well as the impromptu not-at-all-practised-and-with-no-ending sort of show! So we had this simple idea of how to take a show to the road and increase precious time spent outdoors. You can do this activity in a park or just in your back garden.*

**AGE** Any
**TIME** Any
**TOOLS** Clothes pegs, sharp fabric scissors
**MATERIALS** Large old bed sheet (or two smaller ones), long piece of rope, string or twine, ribbon for tying back the curtains

## Step 1

Find an area where two trees are reasonably close together. Tie the length of string or rope between them using a timber hitch knot (see page 19). The area between these trees will be the width of your stage so make sure it is big enough to suit your needs. Now fold over your sheet and peg it to the line so that it hangs all the way to the ground.

## Step 2

Ask a grown-up to help with this bit. Find the middle of your sheet and, with scissors, make a straight cut all the way up, cutting through both sides of the sheet at the same time if you can. Be careful not to cut through your string or rope when you get to the top. Alternatively, you can use two smaller sheets so that no cutting is needed.

## Step 3

Separate the two 'curtains' on the rope and tie them back with twine, ribbon or strips cut from the sheet. Now you are ready to perform your play!

### More ideas

- Decorate your sheet with fabric marker pens to make it really creative or write out the name of your theatre.
- Tie the string a bit lower so that puppets can peep over the top of the sheet with the performers crouched behind it, reaching upwards.
- Make cardboard props like swords, animals or a rocket ship to help bring it all alive – the world is yours to create.
- Do this at home too and make a shadow show. Use lamps from both behind and in front of the sheet to make a shadow show.

# Garden memories

*By Simon Naish*

THE GARDEN OF MY CHILDHOOD WAS A SAFE, BOUNDLESS KINGDOM. I LOOKED AT MY SURROUNDINGS AS A RAINFOREST, THE BEDS OF SOIL AND EARTH AS BARREN DESERTS, HILLS AS MOUNTAIN PEAKS, THE LAND WHERE THE WILD THINGS HAD THEIR WILD RUMPUS. THE EARTH WAS WARM AND HEAVILY SCENTED, THE SKY SO VERY HIGH ABOVE. THE SURROUNDING FLORA KNEW OF NO CURRICULUM OR NEED FOR PAYING MORE ATTENTION. OFTEN I WAS ALONE THERE, THE FRESH SPIDER WEBS BREAKING ACROSS MY FACE, BUT NEVER LONELY.

I had a roller coaster, of course. (A plank resting on the rungs of a long wooden ladder leant against the apple tree.) It was genuinely thrilling – I'd charge my sister's friends one leaf to have a ride. There was no height limit and if the leaf was an unusual colour or shape, you could ride twice.

> *"One long, hot summer, the trench building extended to my cousin's back garden. Or 'Belgium', as we called it."*

Stories of the Grandfather I'd never met who survived the Somme during World War I fuelled the digging of a labyrinth of trenches along the far end of this kingdom. At night, planks would be placed over the defences and mud scattered on top to conceal their existence and prevent enemy occupation.

One long, hot summer, the trench building extended to my cousin's back garden. Or 'Belgium', as we called it. Combined efforts delivered a sizeable trench running the length of the double garden gates, beyond which ran the access gully. The usual camouflaging of the battlements were put in place each night using my uncle's plywood sheets, no doubt destined for something better. We were two young boys bound by the secret of this great toil and that made life good. Towards the end of the school holidays, the trench was significant and proportionate was our joy.

As the shadows lengthened and summer came to an end, I sat filthy and bruised bathing in the kitchen sink after a day of excavation when there came an aggressive knocking at the door. My dad turned down the grilling pikelets to answer it. My uncle stood there, clearly shaken. His face was wearing a strange

> *"We were two young boys bound by the secret
> of this great toil and that made life good."*

expression I'd not seen before. It turned out to be the expression of a man who had decided to park his new car in the back garden. Reversing across a seemingly innocent patch of loose soil behind the garden gates had given rise to a loud cracking noise, followed by a sudden surge backwards and downwards as if the car was being swallowed up by the very earth itself

There were many other tales born of those back gardens, the enchanted places where myth and legend thrive. Nature forges the brightest moments in the setting of our memory.

# Easel tree

*My daughter and I love painting outside, letting nature inspire our artwork. The only issue is that it's quite challenging carrying our bulky easel around with us so that we have something to lean on. We came up with this quick and quirky idea as a solution.*

**AGE** Any
**TIME** 5 minutes+
**TOOLS** A tree, paintbrushes
**MATERIALS** Paints, sheets of paper, duct tape

Why not use a handy tree as your easel when you fancy doing a bit of al fresco painting? Find a suitable tree, one that isn't too wide to accommodate your sheet of paper and not so knobbly that duct tape won't stick to it. Just grab your paper, tape it to the tree and get painting!

## More ideas

- Why not use the tree to do some bark rubbings with crayons too, while you are there?
- Find some leaves, put them in between your paper and the tree and rub over the top to make some leaf rubbings
- You could try to make stick rubbings too; just find some small twigs, put them in between the paper and the tree and rub over the top with a crayon to bring out some cool designs.
- Find some leaves, stick one on with some double-sided sticky tape and create your own woodland person, adding arms and legs, using the leaf as their body or head. Then rub over them with crayons as before.

# Biodegradable bird feeders

*Whatever the weather, our feathered bird friends often need a little help to make sure they are well fed and energized. Not only are these activities a great way to lend a helping hand to nature, but also a fantastic way to learn about local wildlife. Best of all, if you do this in a park, apart from the string/twine, which you will have to collect at a later date, they are entirely biodegradable.*

**AGE** 2+ (younger children will need some assistance)
**TIME** 15 minutes+

## Hanging fruit and nut feeder

**TOOLS** Scissors, apple cutter or knife, darning needle, metal skewer

**MATERIALS** Garden twine, raisins, monkey nuts, apple

### Step 1
First, cut a length of string: about an arm's length will be plenty. Cut up the apple into sections. Using the skewer, carefully make a hole all the way through a piece of apple. Do this slowly as your apple will just break in half if you go too fast. Thread the string through the hole and tie a knot in the end to stop it sliding off.

### Step 2
Do the same for the raisins, nuts and more pieces of apple in any order you like until you have almost filled up the string. Lastly, tie a loop on to the end of your string with any excess you have and hang it up.

1

2

## Simple seedy bird treats

**TOOLS** Scissors, apple corer
**MATERIALS** An apple, pumpkin or sunflower seeds, string, a small stick

### Step 1
Cut a length of string as long as your forearm. Tie one end of the string around the middle point of the small stick; an overhand knot (see page 17) will work fine. The birds will use this to perch on when they are eating.

### Step 2
Using an apple corer, push a hole through the middle of the apple. Now all you need to do is push the sharp end of your seeds into the flesh of the apple, covering it as much as you can.

### Step 3
Thread the string through the middle of the apple with the stick at the bottom. Make a loop at the top with any excess string and hang up.

1

2

3

# Citrus feeders

**TOOLS** Knife, darning needle, metal spoon, bowl, scissors

**MATERIALS** Garden twine, scissors, 100% peanut butter (no added sugar or palm oil), whole citrus fruit, mixed birdseed

### Step 1

Cut your chosen citrus fruit in half, squeeze out the juice and scoop out the flesh using a metal spoon.

### Step 2

Mix the peanut butter and birdseed (1 tbsp of peanut butter per 1 cup of birdseed) together in a bowl. Spoon the mixture into the empty citrus halves, one spoonful at a time, squishing it all down so that it sticks together.

### Step 3

To hang them up, cut a 1½yd (1.5m) piece of twine and thread it through a darning needle. Poke the needle through the outer skin on one side of the fruit, about ¾in (2cm) down from the top edge, and pull it through, leaving a small tail to tie off into a knot to hold it in place. Leave about 12in (30cm) of string for hanging. Do this twice more, so that you have got three lengths of string attached around the fruit. Tie the three strings together at the top and hang up in the garden or at the park, then announce to the birds that dinner is ready!

### Tip

*I find the type of feeder I choose to make will depend on what I have been using. So if I'm making orange juice, I'll make orange feeders from the leftover skin. If I'm making cakes with lemon juice in, the skins will make it to the garden as feeders and so on, so as not to create any additional waste.*

1

2

3

# Fat balls

**TOOLS** Bowl, grater
**MATERIALS** Lard, birdseed (two parts dry seed to one part lard), length of string approx. 18in (45cm), a small stick

### Step 1
Put the birdseed in a bowl and add double the amount of lard. If the lard is solid and hard, use a grater to make it easier to mix in. Mix together with your hands until handfuls of mixture hold together solidly when pressed tightly.

### Step 2
Tie one end of the string around the middle point of a small stick; an overhand knot (see page 17) will work fine. The birds will use this stick to perch on when they are eating.

### Step 3
Now pick up big handfuls of your mixture and squeeze it on to your string, just above the stick. Keep adding, squishing and squeezing until you make a big lump of bird food.

### Step 4
Using the excess string at the top, make a loop to hang it up.

### Tip
*If you make a large batch of birdseed fat balls, you can freeze any extra mixture until they are needed. In very warm weather, the fats can become rancid, so during the summer keep them in a cool shady spot.*

### Variation
You can make a vegan variation if you like. Instead of using lard you can use coconut oil to the same ratio (one part birdseed to two parts oil).

You can make fat balls without string to sit on the top of bird tables, or why not try to make a rustic willow hanging ball (see page 50) and pop a fat ball inside for the birds to enjoy?

1

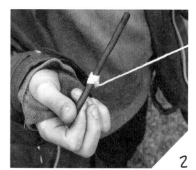
2

3

4

# Honey bee water station

**AGE** Any
**TIME** 5 minutes
**TOOLS** Acrylic
paint pens (optional)
**MATERIALS**
Smooth pebbles,
glass, ceramic or
terracotta plant
pot, shallow dish or
bowl, fresh water

*Honey bees are like miniature superheroes. They fly at a speed of around 16 miles per hour (25kph) and beat their wings 200 times per second, which is pretty cool. They help keep us all alive by making sure our plants and flowers grow, so we can eat! This simple water station takes minutes to assemble, but will help these amazing creatures to survive.*

Choose a spot in the garden that is protected and shady. Place a plant pot upside down. This is the base of the bath. Set the shallow dish or bowl on top of the pot. Choose a plant pot made of glass, ceramic or terracotta, as plastics and metals may leech into the water, making it less safe for the bees to drink. Put a few pebbles into the dish. Add just enough water so that the tops of the stones are not submerged. Change the water daily and clean the bee bath out weekly.

## Tip
*You could decorate the stones if you like. I use acrylic paint pens to make my stones colourful and inviting.*

## Why do bees need water?
- They use it to dilute their honey to make it the right consistency and thin out honey that has crystallized.
- Water helps with their digestion.
- They need it to keep the hive cool. They add water to the hive and fan it with their wings, cooling it down. The bee babies need it too! The nurse bees that feed the larvae need lots of water to create the right baby food (this is called royal jelly).

# Snail race

*My dad recently told me that this was one of his favourite childhood pastimes. Have a good look at your racing snail before you start and work out its distinguishing features so you don't forget which is yours. Give them a name, draw up a leader board, then ready, set, GO!*

**AGE** Any
**TIME** Any
**TOOLS** None
**MATERIALS** Racing surface, duct tape, snails or woodlice

Think where your snails may be hiding. Under rocks or logs? In the vegetable patch, perhaps? It's a good idea to make a note of where you found them so that you can put them back when you're finished.

Mark out the start and finish line using duct tape. Keep an eye on your racing snail but make sure no one else is cheating meanwhile! We used a little coffee table and did the race in the kitchen. It's a great indoor or outdoor activity.

When everyone is ready place your snail on the start line and let them race! Congratulate your mini beast with a micro high five and put it back where you found it.

## Tip
*We found that once we had collected our snails (in a box with a few holes in the lid and a couple of leaves to make them feel at home) they were a little shy and took a while to come out of the shells. We used tiny bits of banana to try and entice them out and this worked beautifully. We also added a tiny bit of water to keep it nice and damp. If you find your snails on a cold day, why not take them inside to warm up a little and race them there? You might find they speed up when they're not so cold!*

# Botanical interactive art

*Art exists everywhere you look and you can even create your own outdoor art collage by collecting the materials you need from the natural world around you. Wouldn't it be fun to not only make the art but be part of it too? This activity inspires you to create a botanical masterpiece and then step right into it! You can be as silly or surreal as you like.*

**AGE** Any
**TIME** Any
**TOOLS** Your imagination
**MATERIALS** Anything from sticks and stones to leaves and pine cones and anything else you find along the way

Explore your chosen location. It could be a park, a grassy verge, your backyard or anywhere else you can think of. Take a look at all the nature growing or living in that area. Find an appropriate place to create your art. Don't use a well-trodden pathway as you may find your art being disturbed before you're finished.

Start to collect materials to create your botanical masterpiece. Depending on your location, these materials will vary. You could use pebbles, small rocks, sticks, leaves, pine cones, acorns, dandelions, daisies, leaves and anything else you come across.

This is really now all down to you and your imagination. There are no rules in land art. Play with creating illusions with size. We had fun creating hats and umbrellas to lie next to and become part of the artwork. Let your imagination run wild!

## More ideas
- Take a photo. It's not likely to be there next time you visit.
- Use small sticks for the outlines and then fill in with coloured leaves and flowers.
- Create a self-portrait and then lie down next to it.
- Make a pair of wings and then 'fly' away with them.
- Make something to rest on your outstretched palm as if you were holding it. It could be anything, from a representation of the Earth to a little bug.
- Make a cup and teapot and lie down next to it to pour it out.
- Make a big piece of cake (or even a whole one) and lie down next to it with your mouth wide open to take a giant bite.
- Make an oversized spider and lie down next to it in a running-away position.

# Giant bubbles

**AGE** Any
**TIME** 10 minutes
**TOOLS** Scissors
**MATERIALS**
Bubble mixture
(see box opposite),
2 garden bamboo
canes, 2 lengths of
string, 1yd (1m) and
2yd (2m) long, two
metal washers

*There's nothing more pleasing than watching giant bubbles blow in the wind on a sunny day. Add in a few happy children trying to chase and pop them, and you've got a great recipe to spend a joyful afternoon outdoors.*

### Step 1

Make a batch of bubble mixture, following the recipe in the box opposite. Tie each end of the shorter length of string to one end of each cane using a clove hitch knot (see also page 16).

### Step 2

Thread both the washers on to the longer length of string. They will act as a weight to create the triangle shape of the giant bubble wand. Slide them into the centre by holding the two ends of the string together. Tie an overhand knot (see page 17) over the washers to keep them in place.

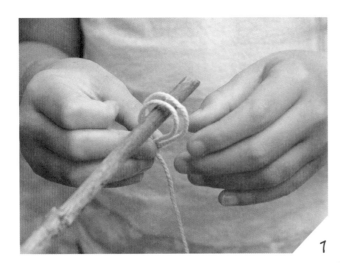

## Step 3

Tie each end of the longer string on to the ends of the canes using an overhand knot so that they are touching where the shorter string has already been tied on. The string should now have formed a big loop with the canes acting as the handles to hold on to.

## Step 4

Dip the string into your pre-made bubble mixture and away you go!

## Tip

*Try to use the bubbles in the shade as the sun tends to dehydrate them and they can pop more easily.*

## Super-strong bubble mixture recipe

- 6 cups water – distilled is best, but tap water is fine too
- 1 cup washing-up liquid
- ½ cup cornflour
- 1 tbsp baking powder (not baking soda)
- 1 tbsp glycerine (found in the baking section at the supermarket)

In a large bowl, dissolve the cornflour in the water, stirring really well. Stir in the rest of the ingredients, being very careful. You don't want the mixture to bubble up yet, so try not to create a lot of froth. Allow the bubble mixture to sit for at least an hour, stirring occasionally when you see the cornflour settling at the bottom. You may need to keep stirring while using your bubble mixture as the cornflour sometimes sinks to the bottom.

4

# Bubble snake maker

**AGE** Any

**TIME** 10 minutes to make – hours of play time

**TOOLS** Scissors, shallow bowl or plate

**MATERIALS** Small empty plastic bottles, bubble mixture (see page 39 for recipe), water, food colouring (optional), an old facecloth or sock, elastic band

*This is a simple way to have great fun outdoors. Using just a few household ingredients, you've got the recipe for hours of fun (well, 30 minutes at least!) And we all know, bubbles are loved by any age.*

### Step 1
Find small empty plastic bottles in your recycling bin and, using the scissors, carefully cut off the bottom.

### Step 2
If you are using a facecloth, cut it into a circular shape to cover the open end of the bottle and secure in place with an elastic band. If you are using an old sock, slide it over the open end of the bottle and secure with an elastic band.

### Step 3
Place the bubble mixture into a shallow bowl or plate. If you would like coloured bubble snakes, drop a couple of drops of food colouring into the mixture.

1

2

**Tip**
*Blowing slowly produces the longest snakes. Be aware of the wind!*

3

4

## Step 4

This part can be a bit messy so do it outside and wear old clothes. Dip the fabric in the bubble solution and gently blow into the bottle at the drinking end.

DO NOT inhale!

After each blow, take the snake maker away from your mouth as you take a breath in to blow another long snake.

## Snake maker bubble mixture

- 3 tbsp washing-up liquid
- 9 fl oz (250ml) water (distilled is best, but tap water is fine too)
- 1 tbsp glycerine (found in the baking section at the supermarket)

Mix all the ingredients together in a bowl, carefully so it doesn't froth up. It works best if you are able to leave it overnight before using, so make it the day before if you can.

# Nature weaving

*Weaving is a great way to explore the textures and colours found in nature. It offers a way to make art, have some quiet time and keeps little hands busy. One of the things I love about this activity is that it is easy enough for pre-schoolers but older children will enjoy it too. The older they are, the more advanced and intricate the weave can be. The finished masterpieces look great hanging up in the house or even displayed outside.*

**AGE** 3+

**TIME** 30 minutes+

**TOOLS** Scissors, secateurs

**MATERIALS** Sticks, plants and herbs from the garden like lavender, or flowers and plants growing in the grass such as daisies, dandelions, plantain etc. Thick cardboard (a minimum of 6 x 6in/15 x 15cm), tape and yarn or string

### Step 1

First create the loom to weave your natural materials into. Take the thick cardboard and cut small slits along two opposite edges. They need to be big enough to keep the yarn in place, about ³⁄₈in (1cm) deep and ³⁄₈in (1cm) between each cut, down the length of the card.

### Step 2

Using a piece of yarn, start at one end of the card and begin wrapping the yarn round and round the card, tucking it into the slits as you go. Leave a 2in (5cm) tail hanging out to tie off at the end and secure each end with a piece of tape. You are now ready to weave.

1

2

3

## Step 3

Gather up materials to weave into your loom such as long grass and flowers. Weave each piece over and under the yarn from one end to the other. It's nice to be able to fill your loom but equally as effective with just a few pieces. Remember, if you started threading over your string you will need to start weaving the next one by going under the string.

### Variations

You can also make a loom out of sticks by lashing four sticks together into a square (see page 17 for shear lashing instructions or just use elastic bands if it is too tricky). Create the strings using yarn secured at the top of the frame and then loop the yarn all the way to the bottom horizontal stick. Continue along the frame until it is filled. Each time you wrap the yarn around either the top or bottom rung you need to do a full turn of the yarn to make it an effective loom. Weave in your foraged materials as before.

# OUTDOOR GAMES

*Playing games provides opportunities for learning and development, and research has shown it can build brain power, increase your fitness, develop confidence, leadership skills and teamwork, and even help improve your marks in school! It's also a fun way to spend time with friends. So find a park, invite some friends and play!*

## Outdoor bowling

Fill the empty water bottles. We used waste plastic packaging, crisp packets and plastic bags but you could use water or sand. These bottles will be the pins. Arrange the bottles in a triangle. Take turns to bowl and keep score. The player who scores the maximum points within a designated time wins the challenge.

**AGE** 2+
**TIME** 10 minutes+
**MATERIALS** 5–10 empty plastic bottles, plastic wrappers, packets, bags, sand or water (optional), a ball
**NUMBER OF PLAYERS** 2+

## Follow the drum

This is more of sensory activity than a game, but very enjoyable. Each person takes a turn to be the noise-maker. Everyone else is blindfolded. Jumpers, scarves or bandanas work just fine. The noise-maker stands about 100yd (100m) away from the group and bangs the drum, or whatever noise-maker they have. The group must then follow the noise. When they are close, the noise-maker can now find a new spot and silently move there, sparking the senses of the group to follow. Swap so that everyone has a chance to try out being a noise-maker. Always be respectful of other people using the park.

**AGE** 4+
**TIME** 5 minutes+
**MATERIALS**
A noise-maker (drum/bells/sticks or stones banged together, etc.)
**NUMBER OF PLAYERS** 3+

## Navigation straight line

It is a fact that when blindfolded, humans cannot walk in a straight line. Try out this theory with this activity. Choose a tree or any landmark. Walk out 50 paces away from the landmark to make a start line. Now, one person in the pair must put on a blindfold (a bandana, jumper or scarf works fine). The sighted player gets on to the back of the blindfolded player, piggy-back style. The blindfolded player now must find their way back to their chosen landmark and stop only when they believe they are have got there.

Variation: if a piggy-back carry is not possible, just place a hand on their shoulder but only lightly. They must not lead or direct them in any way, just reassure them they are not alone.

**AGE** 7+
**TIME** 10 minutes+
**MATERIALS**
A blindfold
**NUMBER OF PLAYERS** Any number of pairs

# Shadow painting

**AGE** Any
**TIME** Any
**TOOLS** None
**MATERIALS** Large pieces of paper, paints, pens, pencils, chalks, any other objects for making shadows with

*Our daughters love to play games with their shadows. Jumping on my shadow and shadow tag are two of their favourites. If you enjoy these too, you may already know that the sun's position in the sky affects the size and shape of our shadows. This activity makes use of shadows to create some fabulous art. It is best done in a wide open space on a very sunny day with no clouds in the sky. Have a play and let the sun be your guide!*

Lay your paper down on the ground. Find a good shadow. It could be from a tree, a person, or anything else you can see. You could even ask someone to hold an interesting, curvy branch over your paper. Play around until you get a good shadow and then carefully trace the outline. You can then fill your picture in using paints or big chalks.

## Why not make your own chalk paint?
- ½ cup cornflour
- ½ cup water
- Food colouring

Mix equal parts cornflour and water, stir together and add a few drops of food colouring to your desired vibrancy. If you have a sludge of cornflour in the bottom of your paint cup, just add more water and stir.

Now you've got your very own paint to use outside on all of your sunny creations. Just be aware that these could stain clothes, so wear old clothes or an apron.

## More ideas

- Experiment by looking at shadows at different times throughout the day. Is the morning best or just as the sun goes down? Record your findings in your nature journal (see page 108).
- Create shadows with your body or different objects of different shapes and sizes.
- Use chalks or chalk paint (see box opposite) directly on to a pavement or driveway. The rain does a fabulous washing-up job. Just remember, not everyone likes their driveway covered in chalk so it's best to check first.

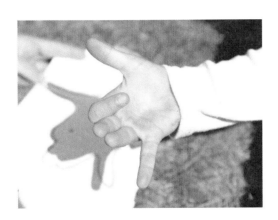

# Fizzy mud pies

*Most children love to play in the mud. Given half a chance they would probably cover themselves from head to toe in the stuff! Mud soup making, a full-on mud café serving muddy spaghetti, a cake-making factory, mud art: the possibilities are endless! Muddy play is a great antidote to our overly sanitized lives and can even be good for a child's immune system, by exposing them to beneficial bacteria and microbes in the soil. These fizzing pies will be a popular addition to their mud-making repertoire.*

**AGE** Any
**TIME** 10 minutes preparation
**TOOLS** Mixing bowl, spoon, old mugs, any other mud-kitchen equipment
**MATERIALS** Soil, small amount of sand for texture and water to make mud, bicarbonate of soda, vinegar decanted into a squirty bottle, paper cupcake cases, powdered paints, food colouring or grated chalk for colouring the pies

## Mess warning!

This activity can be very messy so I would highly recommend old clothes and aprons.

## Step 1

Mix the soil, sand and water together until you have the desired consistency of mud. Now add in bicarbonate of soda until you have a ratio of 1:3 parts bicarbonate of soda to mud. Mix together well. If you need to, add some more water to make a gooey, cake-like mixture.

## Step 2

It's good to just use small portions of your mud at a time. Once the mud is all mixed up, it will still look just like plain old mud. Play around with cupcake cases to make little muffins and old mugs to make teas and coffees.

## Playing with mud ideas

Playing with mud can be so much fun and although mud pies are an absolute favourite, there's plenty more you can do. Just make sure you wear old clothes and have a bucket of water outside ready for cleaning up.

- Buy some ice-cream cones and create a thick mud. Use real ice-cream scoops to get the right shape and sprinkle on grated chalk for colour and sticks for chocolate flakes.

- Make a really wet mixture and spread a thin layer over a flat outdoor surface – pavements or sheets of cardboard work well. Use sticks like a pencil to draw a design and make muddy art.

- Mix your mud up to a super-thick and wet mixture. Take off your shoes and socks and get stomping in the mud. Walk across large pieces of paper and make muddy tracks.

- With a very thick mixture and a mould, try to make bricks and then dry them out. See if you can build with these later to make a little house.

- Using a thick, sticky mixture, make doughnuts with petals or grated chalk for sprinkles.

- Or, do the ultimate... paint your body with mud and turn yourself into a muddy monster. Make sure you check with a grown-up first that a muddy monster coming through the house for a wash is OK with them!

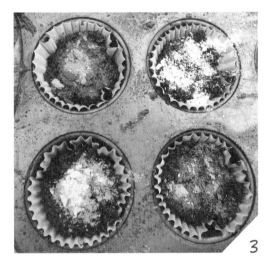

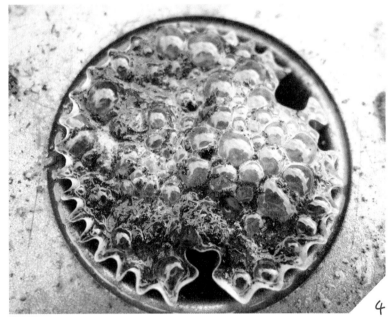

## Step 3

If you want to add colour, you can sprinkle on grated chalk or powered paints or add a few drops of food colouring on top of your creations.

## Step 4

Now for the magic part. Add a few squirts of vinegar to your muddy pies and watch for a fizzy reaction!

## Tip

*Instead of mud, try playing with old coffee or tea granules. They make great mud pies too!*

## Mobile mud pit

If your garden isn't particularly muddy, why not make a mobile mud pit using a large tub or tray? You can buy a big bag of topsoil from a local garden centre and mix it with water and some sand for added texture. Even if you have a garden space with plenty of mud, I recommend having a designated area for muddy play, especially if you have flowers or veggies growing in your garden. That way you can experiment with your mud, adding paint and other fun ingredients without covering the rest of your outdoor space.

# A city camping adventure

*by Jessica Smith*

I'VE FOUND THAT LIVING IN THE CITY FORCES YOU TO INTERACT WITH NATURE IN AN ENTIRELY DIFFERENT WAY; YOU HAVE TO SEEK IT OUT, SEARCH FOR WILD SPACES TO GET YOUR FIX OR, IF POSSIBLE, CREATE YOUR OWN. TRY DIPPING TOES INTO A STREAM IN THE PARK, NOTICING THE TREES IN THE LOCAL PARK AND IMAGINING THE ANIMAL FOLK THAT MIGHT LIVE THERE, LOOKING FOR SIGNS OF CREATURES AND SPOTTING THEIR DENS OR NESTS, UP HIGH AND DOWN BELOW.

We're very blessed that, even though we live in London, our garden has provided a wealth of wild and unexpected experiences for us to enjoy nature; from acrobatic squirrels back-flipping and raiding the birdfeeders, to frogs greeting us at the back door. Foxes gracefully chase each other in the early morning and steal the odd shoe from the back door, only to frustratingly return someone else's or a tattered and torn version in its place.

As a family, we value outside experiences and being connected to nature so living in a city, we try to take up every opportunity to share this with our daughter. We have planted fruit trees and edibles in the garden to connect our kitchen to the garden and ensure there is always something interesting to watch grow, pick and cook with. Currently, there are hundreds of tiny budding apples ready for a bumper crop of apple sauces, crumbles and other apple delicacies, a new blueberry bush is beginning to fruit and the wild garlic edging the garden is starting to die back for the season.

Recently, my daughter and I tested out a new tent by pitching it in the back garden and spending the night there. Being so close to home meant we could deck out the tent with every blanket and cushion going; a palatial room of cosiness. At the same time, we got to enjoy lighting a fire, toasting marshmallows and listening out for the rustles, creaks, tweets, squeaks and scratches as we snoozed under canvas. Having frequent fox visitors to the garden we were curious to see and hear their nightly adventures from close quarters. My daughter loved the sounds and the elongated shadows of trees cast on our walls for the night. Every sound could be a story, unseen and mysterious,

*"Foxes gracefully chase each other in the early morning and steal the odd shoe from the back door, only to frustratingly return someone else's"*

*"Being so close to home meant we could deck out the tent with every blanket and cushion going"*

echoing in our fascinated minds. We stayed up late, forced to sleep according to the slow dimming of spring light and, thankfully, did not wake too early as the tent was shaded by a sycamore tree that borders our garden. Breakfast was taken in the tent and even the family cat came along to join in for hot chocolate and toast.

It truly reminded me that a garden, of any size, in any place, gives rise to a wealth of opportunities to engage with nature and its cycles. It's about creating the opportunities to enjoy nature that suit you best or even just trying to stop to notice them once in a while.

# Willow hanging ball

*This attractive ball can be used for lots of different things. You can hang battery-powered LED tea lights in it as a simple way to decorate your doorstep or garden, or even hang bird food inside it. Remember, it is supposed to be rustic, so don't worry about it looking neat and tidy.*

**AGE** 6+ (will need adult assistance with the initial wreath-making stage)
**TIME** 40 minutes+
**TOOLS** Secateurs, scissors
**MATERIALS** approximately 30–40 willow rods 3ft (1m) long, garden twine, yarn (optional)

### Step 1
Start by making 3–4 willow rings. We will call these 'wreaths'. Start with the thicker ends of the rods and finish with the thinner. Take your first rod and weave it into a rustic hoop, about the diameter you want your final ball to be, leaving a tail piece sticking out. These will all get cut and tidied up at the end.

### Step 2
Add another rod to the wreaths, starting a quarter turn away from your first, again leaving the tail sticking out for the time being. Add a few more rods to each wreath in the same way. It helps to think about your wreath like a clock with the first stick starting at 12 o'clock, the second stick starting at quarter past, the third at half past and the fourth at quarter to.

### Step 3
Snip off any untidy ends with the secateurs.

### Step 4
Once you have 3–4 wreaths all the same size, you are ready to assemble the ball. Slip one wreath over the other to start building the ball shape, making a cross shape at either end. Tie the first two circles together at the top. You can tie a little knot to secure the bottoms too. They will be cut off at the end so don't worry about making your knots neat. You can add another wreath in the same way if you like, but this is optional.

### Step 5
For your final wreath, slip it over the top down to the middle, like a belt holding all your other wreaths in place. This will create the three-dimensional structure.

### Step 6
Once the rings are all in place you can start filling in the gaps. You can use further lengths of willow to weave in and out of your ball, tucking the ends in wherever they reach, or use yarn to give it the look that you want, tying the strands off randomly. Remember, it's a rustic ball so don't worry about making it completely neat. Don't forget that if you want to put something into your ball like a fat ball for the birds or a tea light, leave a bit of a gap somewhere so that you can place the fat ball inside.

### Step 7
Add a little string hanging loop at the top and hang wherever you like – for you, for the birds or for the garden.

### Where to find willow
You need willow for this activity. If you are lucky enough to have access and permission to cut living willow sticks from a tree, that's great. Use your secateurs and cut 3ft (1m) lengths of thin willow sticks. You'll need to strip the leaves off before you start to weave. If you do not have access to a tree, there are plenty of willow suppliers online that you can order it from.

## How to soak dried willow

If you buy dried willow (often referred to as rods) you will need to soak these to rehydrate before you can use them. Using a bath is fine. The general rule is one day of soaking per 1ft (30cm) of willow. For example, if your willow was 3ft (1m) long, it would need three days to soak. After it is soaked, leave it outside under a damp sheet and a tarpaulin overnight to help make it super supple.

1

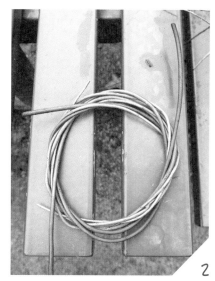

2

3

4

5

6

7

# Sheet dens

*Making indoor sheet forts, cushion slides and blanket castles to hide in for hours on end is a favourite pastime for many children, but why stick to making them indoors? Pack your sheets into a bag and head to the local park, or into your garden, if you have one. Here are three tried-and-tested methods for making outdoor sheet dens.*

**AGE** Any
**TIME** 10 minutes+
**TOOLS** Scissors, tent pegs (optional)
**MATERIALS** Spare large bedding sheets, string, rope, small stones, duct tape (optional), fallen branches

## Tip
*Attach a piece of duct tape to each corner of the sheet, back and front. With a pair of scissors, carefully cut a small hole. You can use these with tent pegs later on if needed.*

## The tent

Find two trees that are close together. Tie a length of rope between them at about chest height. Use a quick-release slip knot at one end and a timber hitch at the other (see pages 18 and 19). Now drape your sheet over the rope with half hanging either side to form a tent shape. You can peg down the corners of the sheet using rocks, or fallen branches, if you can find any. Or, alternatively, use tent pegs.

# The hanging castle

Find an area with at least one tree with low-hanging branches. If you can find a handful of small stones that would help with this design, but it can be done without.

Spread the sheet out on the ground. If you have some small stones, place them underneath the sheet in various areas, spread out where you would like the sheet to be suspended from. Gather each stone into the sheet and tie a length of string around the base so that the stone is completely enclosed in the fabric. Finish off with an overhand knot (see page 17), leaving a tail about 1yd (1m) long.

If you don't have any stones, just use your string to wrap around small gathered sections of the sheet, tying them off with an overhand knot and leaving a long tail, as before.

Use the long strings to secure the sheet to the low-hanging branches of the tree. The sheet will drape and create a shelter. Peg out with larger rocks, fallen branches or tent pegs.

### Tip
*Use fabric pens or acrylic paint pens to create your own designs on your sheets first.*

## The stand-alone

You will need to find three fallen branches. One should, ideally, be as tall as you are. The other two can be more like the length of your shoulder to your fingertip. Lash the two smaller branches together using the string (see page 17) and open up to form an upside-down V-shape, with a small fork at the top just above the knot. Place on the ground, and balance the longer branch with one end resting into the fork at the top and the other end on the ground. This will create the skeleton of your shelter. You can lash the three sticks together at the top to secure. Throw over the sheet to create a shelter.

### Tip
*If you want a bigger fort, use two large sheets, pegged together with clothes pegs.*

### Leave no trace
Don't forget to carefully dismantle your shelter and take everything home with you, even if you plan to come back and play the next day. We need to respect our public spaces and leave nothing behind.

# Nature's board games

*I love old-fashioned, traditional games. Despite so many new games being invented on both board and screen, the old ones just seem to stick around, being passed down to each younger generation. I'll bet your grandparents played these games when they were children. Why not take these old favourites to a new level and try to recreate them just using sticks and stones outside?*

## Pebble tic-tac-toe

Rivers are an especially great place for pebble foraging as the river tends to help with the smoothing process.

### Step 1

Find 10 smooth roundish pebbles. Decide on the symbols to paint on your pebbles. You can be traditional and, using acrylic paint pens, paint five crosses and five circles or be creative and try ladybirds, leaves, bees or flowers. There are no rules here!

### Step 2

Draw the grid onto the piece of felt. Using a ruler, mark out nine even boxes. Each square should measure 2 x 2in (5 x 5cm). Draw two lines running vertically and two running horizontally.

**AGE** 4+
**TIME** 10 minutes, plus playing time
**TOOLS** Ruler
**MATERIALS** Acrylic paint pens, 10 small, smooth pebbles, a piece of felt or leather 6 x 6in (15 x 15cm)
**PLAYERS** 2

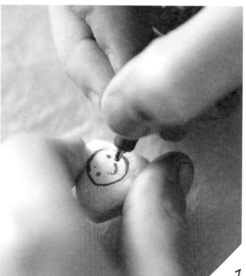

1

2

## Tic-tac-toe on the go

Create a grid using four sticks of a similar length criss-crossing over each other. Decide which player will play with which set of items. Take it in turns to place an item in the empty squares of the grid. The aim is to try to get three in a row (diagonally, across or down) and to block the other player from doing the same.

**AGE** 4+
**TIME** 10 minutes+
**TOOLS** None
**MATERIALS** Four sticks roughly the same size (minimum 12in/30cm in length), two sets of five items that are all the same (but different to the other set) to play with, for example, small sticks, stones, leaves or flowers
**PLAYERS** 2

## Snakes and ladders

**AGE** 6+
**TIME** 20 minutes+
**TOOLS** A dice
**MATERIALS** Long sticks (about 3ft/1m long), lots of smaller sticks to create ladders and a few bright leaves from the ground to be the snakes
**PLAYERS** 2+

The original playing board has 100 squares but you do not have to make yours this big. I would suggest 20 squares minimum, in rows of five, but this is up to you. Go bigger if you have enough sticks.

Add your snakes (overlapping leaves), placing each one so that it leads from one square down to another, diagonally or directly up or down.

Make your ladders. Using the smaller sticks create ladders both big and small, leading from one square up to another.

Now all that's left to do is play. Roll the dice and try to get to the final square. If you stand in a square that has a ladder in it, follow it up to the square it sits in. If you stand in a square with a snake, bad news; travel back down the board to where the snake begins. Remember, if you roll a six, you get another turn. Try to get to the end (with the board still intact!).

# Track traps

*This activity is great for finding out more about what lurks, creeps or scuttles around when we're not looking. Do you have hedgehogs in your garden or maybe a local mouse or rat? One of the best clues they could leave behind is their tracks. Lay down one of these creature-friendly track traps to find out more. And for those of you without gardens, no problem, you can take this activity to a park or local green space. Become a nature detective on tour! Just remember to take whatever you take there home with you.*

**AGE** 5+ (with assistance)

**TIME** 30 minutes +

**TOOLS** Ruler, pencil, metal skewer, paintbrush, PVA glue or glue stick, scissors, teaspoon

**MATERIALS** 100% pure peanut butter (or cat or dog food), A3 (tabloid size) black mount board or A3 black fluted plastic board (available online, approx. ⅛in (4mm) thick), 1 sheet of A4 (letter size) white paper, a small piece of cloth or greaseproof paper, 1 tsp olive oil, non-toxic black poster paint, garden twine

### Tip
*You can use robust cardboard for this project but it won't last too long, especially if it gets wet. Fluted plastic board is much stronger and the corrugated plastic sheet will be waterproof, which means you can use it again and again.*

### Step 1
Divide the card or plastic sheet into thirds lengthways and score down the lines with a pencil and ruler a few times, depending on how thick your material is.

### Step 2
Fold up the two outer strips so that the outer edges meet at the top. It should be a triangular shape, flat on the bottom with the two sides meeting at the top, creating a ridge.

### Step 3
Make three holes along each side of the top edges, at even intervals. One on each end and one in the middle should be enough. You can make these holes by poking through a metal skewer but keep your fingers away from the back of the hole! Make sure that the holes match up on each side.

### Step 4
Glue the white paper to fit along the bottom of the triangular tunnel. You will need to cut it to fit.

### Step 5
Lay the bait (the peanut butter, dog or cat food) down in a horizontal line in the middle of the white paper.

### Step 6
Using your paintbrush, dab on generous blobs of non-toxic poster paint mixed with a teaspoon of olive oil on to cloth or folded-up greaseproof paper at the ends. These will act as your 'ink pads'.

### Step 7
Tie the top of the trap together using the three pairs of holes you made earlier and the garden twine.

### Step 8
Now all that's left to do is find the perfect spot in your garden or park to leave the trap overnight (a). Somewhere private is best rather than a well-used pathway. As long as you leave it somewhere out of the way in a park and come back for it in the morning that should be OK. You could always put a little sign saying 'Do not disturb, nature detective work in progress', so that members of the public do not try to pick it up. Check the paper in the morning for any prints (b).

### Tip
*Try to keep a journal of your results so that you can refer back to them later. Maybe you have a local rodent that keeps coming back for more, or maybe you have different tracks each time? You could draw or photograph your findings and stick them in your nature journal (see page 108).*

**AGE** 3+
**TIME** 20 minutes
**TOOLS** Garden trowel or large spoon, two small plates or a dish
**MATERIALS** Baking tray, sand, water, fruits, veggies and nuts

# Variation: basic track trap

This is a slightly easier version for your backyard or garden: a simple project for all ages that uses supplies you probably already have at home. You can do this project over and over again, just smooth over the sand and refill when necessary.

### Step 1

Scoop enough sand into the baking tray to cover the bottom completely. Add a small amount of water to dampen it. Smooth the sand over using the garden trowel. You can test it by gently placing your finger on an area of the sand. If it leaves a mark, great, you're ready to smooth over again and continue.

If you can't see any marks, just add a little more water and test again.

### Step 2

Now add your bait. Put the fruit or veggies into a small shallow dish. In another, add water. Place these dishes on the tray in the middle, to encourage animals to walk on the sand.

### Step 3

Place the trap in a quiet spot in your yard, garden or even somewhere in your local park or green space. Leave the trap overnight. Check the trap for tracks in the morning.

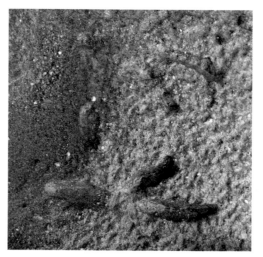

### Tip
*You never know, you might even be lucky enough to get extra clues. Visitors might not just leave their tracks, they might also leave their scat (which is the nice way of saying poo!) Don't be totally grossed out, it's a great new clue.*

# Identify your tracks

Now all that is left to do is to identify your tracks. Here are a few to get you started:

Fox

Mole

Rat

Cat

Hedgehog

Pigeon

Squirrel

Badger

Mouse

# Around the city or town

YOU CAN FIND NATURE ALMOST ANYWHERE – YOU JUST
NEED TO GO OUT AND LOOK FOR IT. LOOK UP IN THE SKY TO
SEE BIRDS, FLYING BEASTS AND CLOUDS. WATCH OUT FOR
NATURE PUSHING UP THROUGH CRACKS IN THE PAVEMENT,
OR MOSS COVERING WALLS. LOOK OUT FOR SIGNS OF
CREATURES MAKING THEIR HOMES: WITH WEBS, IN TINY
HOLES IN TREES OR IN THE CREVICES OF BRICKS.
IF YOU SPEND TIME LOOKING, I PROMISE YOU WILL FIND
NATURE SHOWING ITSELF IN ALL SORTS OF WAYS.

# Cloud spotting

**AGE** Any
**TIME** Any
**TOOLS** Pen or pencil
**MATERIALS** Paper

*Have you ever looked up to find clouds in the shape of a particular animal or tried to predict the weather? Looming, grey, rain-filled clouds mean you'll be wearing wellies today, or a total absence of any clouds means sun hats and sunshine. Learn these different types of cloud and then go out and look skywards.*

Do some cloud spotting when you are out and about and collect points for each type you see. Copy out the table below and use the cloud information opposite to identify each one you spot and then write down the details. Do it with a friend and see who can get to 100 first. The beauty is you can do this game in towns, cities, parks, on mountains, in fields or anywhere in the world!

### So what exactly is a cloud?

Water on the Earth evaporates and turns into an invisible gas. This gas then rises up into the sky. Higher up where the air is colder, the water condenses and changes from a gas to drops of water or crystals of ice. We can then see these drops of water as clouds. The drops fall back down to earth as rain, and then the water evaporates again, creating a water cycle.

| Cloud name | Date | Weather outcome | Points to earn | Points gained |
|---|---|---|---|---|
| Cumulus | | | 10 | |
| Altocumulus | | | 20 | |
| Stratocumulus | | | 11 | |
| Stratus | | | 15 | |
| Nimbostratus | | | 25 | |
| Cirrus | | | 15 | |
| Cumulonimbus | | | 30 | |

# Types of clouds

### Cumulus
These are mid-level clouds. They are like giant cotton wool puffs drifting lazily across the sky on a sunny day and are easy to spot. Cumulus clouds are often called 'fair-weather clouds'. Sun hats today!

### Altocumulus
These are mid-level clouds that appear as groups of white or grey puffs, like someone has emptied a jar of cotton wool balls into the sky. If you see altocumulus clouds on a warm, sticky morning, expect to see thunderstorms late in the afternoon.

### Stratocumulus
These form in rolls or ripples in a row, which can be all joined up or with gaps in between, usually blocking out the sun. But good news: even though they can look a bit moody, rain rarely occurs with these clouds.

### Stratus
These are very low clouds and can cover the entire sky like bed sheets throwing an invisibility cloak over the tops of buildings. Often greyish in colour, they are like a fog that doesn't reach the ground. Light mist or drizzle sometimes falls out of these clouds. Maybe a hood is advisable.

### Nimbostratus
These form a dark grey, wet-looking cloudy layer associated with continuously falling rain or snow. Expect rain.

### Cirrus
These are high clouds. They look like wispy feathers, white locks of hair or horses' tails. Cirrus clouds are usually white and predict fair to pleasant weather. When these clouds start to thicken, this is a sign of moisture and a tip to get your wellies on.

### Cumulonimbus
These are thunderstorm clouds and are associated with heavy rain, snow, hail, lightning and even tornadoes. These clouds can sometimes grow to over 10 miles (16km) high! Maybe think about an indoor activity today.

# CITY WILDLIFE SPOTTER

*Many of the same animals that we see in the countryside have also cleverly adapted to life in towns and cities. You may be so used to seeing them that you don't think much about it. How about getting to know them again, relearning their clever ways and giving them due respect as interesting, intelligent, inspiring beings? Swot up on these fascinating facts and watch carefully next time you spot one of these amazing creatures.*

## Squirrels

### Did you know?

Squirrels can smell food under up to 1ft (30cm) of snow! This is particularly useful for stealing their neighbour's stash. Frustratingly for a squirrel, they often lose about 25% of their hard-earned stash to other squirrels in the local area. They sometimes dig holes and then vigorously cover them up again, but without depositing any nuts, just to throw off potential food thieves.

Did you know that a squirrel's front teeth never stop growing?

Have you ever noticed that a squirrel never runs directly across the road when trying to cross in front of a car? This is because when they feel threatened, they run in zigzag patterns to try and confuse predators, such as hawks. This isn't particularly useful for cars that are trying to avoid them.

Do you think that squirrels are kind of cute? Well, have you ever seen a squirrel baby? They are about 1in (2.5cm) long!

### Extra respect

They contribute massively to the planting of new trees, due to the fact that they never find all of their stashed-away nuts. More trees mean clean air, less flooding and oxygen for us to breathe, so thank you squirrels!

### Spotting tips

The best place to spot a squirrel in the city or in a town is in an urban park. Squirrels are drawn there to hide in the trees, eat the seeds and nuts that trees bear and wait for humans to leave scraps from their picnics.

# Foxes

### Did you know?

Foxes are part of the dog family. They are, in fact, a distant relative of the wolf. But, characteristically they behave more like cats. They hunt like cats, stalking and pouncing. They are the only type of dog capable of retracting their claws like cats do. Like cats, a fox has sensitive whiskers and spines on its tongue. It walks on its toes, which accounts for its elegant, cat-like tread. Foxes are the only member of the dog family that can climb trees. They are dogs, but they act like cats.

Foxes are very fast. They can run up to around 40mph (65kph).

Foxes are solitary beings, preferring to live on their own, but they are fantastic parents. The fathers bring food to their young and the mothers stay with them for around seven months. Did you know that a fox is only pregnant for around 50–60 days?

### Extra respect

Foxes are excellent hunters. They use their incredible sense of smell and sight, as well as their amazing speed and agility to catch their prey. By hunting insects, small rodents and rabbits, foxes help to protect farms from pests that can cause damage.

### Spotting tips

Foxes are best spotted at dawn and dusk. They are very territorial and you may have one in your area – look around rubbish bins and under, or around, sheds.

### Encountering a city fox

A few years ago, I took a train to London from my countryside home in Shropshire, UK. When I got off the train, there was a fox just standing there, looking directly at me. It was totally unafraid of me and the other quick-moving, bustling passengers all around. In fact, the other passengers, eager to get on with their journey, seemed to see the fox but not react to it in any way. So I did the same. I also ignored the fox and walked on. I'm not quite sure why.

It felt strange, because in the countryside I would have stopped in my tracks, hoping not to startle the fox. I would have spent some time in awe of the animal, observing it, as long as it remained there. I would have had at least a moment of gratitude, feeling blessed to have had the rare encounter. I suppose, in a city, foxes are an everyday occurrence, but they are fascinating creatures. How about really looking and learning next time you see one?

# Badgers

### Did you know?

Badgers are incredibly clean and will not poop in their underground homes, called a sett. They dig special communal toilets made up of shallow pits placed away from the setts on the edge of their territory. They will not bring food into the sett either. I wonder if they also take their shoes off at the door?

Badgers do not hibernate during winter but instead go into a deep sleep called 'torpor'. During torpor, their body temperature and heartbeat goes down, reserving their energy. Badgers sleep for a day or two, wake up to eat, and sleep some more. A badger may spend much of the winter in cycles of torpor that last around 29 hours.

Badgers can run up to 19mph (30kph) but only for short periods of time. They are also good at climbing, and they can swim too.

The word badger is said to derive from the French *bêcheur*, meaning digger. Badgers learn to hunt for themselves by the time they are four months old and head out on their own at about six months old.

### Extra respect

Watching them foraging for food in your garden or local green space is a special sight. Badgers will also remove some harmful creatures that may damage your crops, fruits or flowers.

### Spotting tips

Gardens are prime foraging areas for badgers. Some people will not want to encourage badgers into their gardens as they can cause damage digging up vegetables and lawns. However, if you do want to extend an invite, you could try leaving out a handful of peanuts. Please be mindful of your neighbours – you might want to welcome badgers into your garden but they might not!

### Jot it down

If you see any of these animals, make a note in your nature journal (see page 108). Where did you see it? When? Did it see you? Try to draw a picture of it using your memory.

## Hedgehogs

### Did you know?

Their young are called 'hoglets'. Each hedgehog has around 5,000–7,000 spines, although I'm not sure I fancy counting them!

These little creatures can run over 6ft (2m) per second and when out foraging in the evening, they can travel up to 2 miles (3.2km). That's a really long way for such little legs, the equivalent of a human travelling around 8-9 miles (12–14km) a day to find food!

Most mammals have fur or hair that is quite flexible and soft but a hedgehog is different. Hedgehogs have a thick layer of spikes known as quills. These quills are made of something called keratin, which is the same stuff our hair and fingernails are made out of.

### Extra respect

They are also well known as the 'gardener's friend'. This is because their staple diet is made up from pests that are common in our back gardens and green spaces, such as beetles and caterpillars. This helps preserve the fruit, flowers and vegetables growing there.

### Spotting tips

Hedgehogs love areas that can provide lots of worms, so football fields at dusk or dawn can be a good bet to try and get a sighting. They also like to hide in woodpiles in gardens, so you could also try making an area in your garden or local park which provides this sort of space and keeping watch at sun up or sun down.

## Pigeons

### Did you know?

Pigeons are amazing at navigation. A champion racing pigeon can be released 400-600 miles (643-965km) away from its home and still return within a day. It isn't just trained pigeons that have this skill; all pigeons have the ability to return to their roost like this.

Have you ever wondered why you don't see baby pigeons? Their babies remain in the nest for up to two months before bidding farewell to their mum and dad. This gives the young pigeon a massive advantage, leaving the nest better equipped to cope on its own and less at risk to the usual predators of young birds.

Some people consider pigeons to be one of our most intelligent birds as they are able to undertake tasks previously thought possible for only humans and primates. A pigeon can recognize its own reflection in a mirror, one of only six species, and the only non-mammal, that has this ability.

### Extra respect

Pigeons were deployed as mail carriers during World War I and World War II. They saved numerous lives by delivering information about the enemy.

### Spotting tips

Where there are people there are pigeons! Naturally, pigeons should feast on grains and seed, with some species eating small insects and fruit. However, in urban areas they rely mainly on humans to feed them, either by choice or indirectly by the food they leave behind.

**AGE** Any
**TIME** Any
**TOOLS** None
**MATERIALS** None

# City sit spot

*Practising a 'sit spot' is about taking a moment to be still, calm your mind and take in your surroundings without trying to be part of it or change it in any way. Sit spots are often done in a natural setting, but they can happen anywhere. A moment observing a city atmosphere, a bustling town, the people, the birds, the insects, the clouds and the smells is just as valuable as it would be in the woods or in a garden. When we stop for a moment, we tune in with our senses, our thoughts and feelings and this can be a very positive experience.*

Find an area that feels right to you. It could be a park bench or town bench. It could be under a tree or outside your front door. Wherever it is, the only rule is that you need to be comfortable.

Choose a time. It really should be 10 minutes or more to get the full effect, but give it whatever time you have. If you like, you can set a timer so you're not constantly looking at a watch. If you do set a timer it might allow you to be in the moment a bit more as you don't need to wonder how long you've been there for or start thinking about whether it's lunchtime yet.

Tip
*Try to do a sit spot once a week or even once a month. Making time to revisit the same spot is important to be able to see the changes that occur from season to season and at different times of the day.*

Now sit. Be still. Try to free your mind of noisy outside thoughts. Take in the sights, the smells and the sounds. It doesn't just have to be of nature – it can be of people too. Sit quietly without moving. Use your peripheral vision if you can (see tip box). There's so much to take in around you, take the time to absorb it. Even close your eyes so you can hear more clearly without distraction.

After your chosen time is up, write about it in your nature journal (see page 108). Note how you feel after taking that time. Did you like it?

## Things to look and listen for

- Are there any tiny spiders making their way around?
- Is there birdsong?
- Are people noisy here?
- Are people busy here?
- Is there any traffic?
- Can you see any trees? Are they moving in any wind? Are their leaves changing colour? Do they even have leaves?
- What can you smell? Is it familiar? Is it nice?
- What colours are around you?
- Put your hands over your ears. Do you see things more clearly?
- Cup your ears with your hands. Can you hear anything further away?

## Peripheral vision

Peripheral or 'side vision' is the ability to see objects and movement outside of your direct line of vision. Try this exercise to find your width of vision. Stand with your arms outstretched in front of you, palms face down. Fix your eyes on a spot in front of you and do not shift your gaze. Start wiggling your fingers and slowly move your arms out to either side, keeping them straight and your gaze fixed. Notice when you can no longer see your wiggling fingers. How far can you see without moving your head?

Do the same again, but now we're going to find your height of vision. Once again, stand with hands and arms outstretched in front of you but this time with your hands sandwiched on top of each other. Now start wiggling your fingers and move your hands and arms with one arm going up and the other going down, making sure you can see your wiggling fingers at all times. Stop when you can no longer see your fingers wiggling. This is how far your peripheral vision can see without moving your head!

# Grass snake

*by Lois Dale*

WHEN MY HUSBAND AND I SAW A GRASS SNAKE JUST BY THE SIDE OF THE ROAD
IN OUR TOWN, IN THE EARLY SUMMER SUNSHINE, IT WAS EXACTLY 30 YEARS SINCE
I HAD SEEN MY FIRST ONE, IN MY CLASSROOM AT PRIMARY SCHOOL.

I remember my wide eyes marvelled at her opalescent beauty, as a kind man held her for us to take a closer look. I remember how my fingers reached out tentatively to stroke her smooth skin, as she gazed calmly at the children around her, with the regal air of one who knows

> *"...she gazed calmly at the children around her, with the regal air of one who knows she holds the rightful sway over her subjects."*

she holds the rightful sway over her subjects. Back then, you think you will always have such chances to see such beings. And yet here we were, all this time later, and I had not seen one in all those years.

My husband and I were pretty sure this was a grass snake, as we knew that slow worms were mostly copper brown, and we'd seen them before. This one was a sort of grey or olive green. And surely it wasn't a viper, because they have dark zigzags down their backs, and are quite small. This one was long, maybe a metre or so, with dark markings all along its

sides, not that we wanted to look too closely. We were pretty sure it wasn't a black mamba as we weren't in Africa, even though they also like being on roads in the sunshine, but best to be careful!

You do get more careful when you get older, and perhaps a bit less likely to see the magic of coming across a snake when you least expect it. And magic it was, as the gleamingly beautiful creature shimmied like a mirage on the road, in the sunshine that came down through the trees at the edge of the road.

My husband and I froze, praying we would not disturb her, so that we could gaze at her just a little bit longer. We held our breath, desperate not to intrude, but then a different kind of desperation came over us, as she uncoiled her way forward, and we realized she was trying to cross the road. We looked at each other in consternation. A car could come around the corner at any time, and there was precious little time to spare!

We drew closer to protect her. My husband knelt, scooping her carefully into the crook of his arm, and then

cradling her so that she could coil around his arm and lean into his chest. I stood in the middle of the road to face what turned out to be mercifully absent traffic, as he walked his new friend across to the other side, for all the world to see, like a gentleman escorting an elegant lady to a dance.

There, he knelt again, and the snake slid gracefully from his arms to the ground. She flashed what I was convinced was a flirtatious eye in his direction, gathered up her coils, like the skirts of a beautiful dress, and flickered away through the undergrowth to safety. We sighed to see her going, we smiled at each other in some relief, and we walked on, the richer for our experience. It is never too late to look around you. You never know what you might see.

# BUG SUPERPOWERS

*They may be small, but do not overlook them. Love them or hate them, bugs and insects play an important role in our day-to-day lives. Whether in a park, garden, playground, town or city, creepy crawlies are everywhere. In fact, they make up more than half of all living things on the planet. Without them, our world would be an entirely different place.*

Insects pollinate many of our fruits, vegetables and flowers, giving us food to eat. Some feed on decaying organic matter from plants and animals; without them to help break it all down our environment would be very messy indeed. Some of them even eat the pesky bugs that destroy our crops, acting like miniature bodyguards to our plants. Insects are also a source of food for many other animals and play an important role in our food chain. Around the world, insects and bugs are also a healthy source of food for lots of people, rich in vitamins and minerals. Yum Yum! Fancy some grasshopper soup?

## Ladybirds

They are super-eaters. As soon as they hatch, they immediately start munching. These little minibeasts can eat up to 5,000 aphids in a lifetime.

They have psychic abilities and can navigate without a sat nav! OK, not quite, but they know when winter is coming, due to the lack of aphids, then they make their way back to their ancestral home and hibernate.

They have an amazing defence superpower. They can give themselves stinky feet! It's true. Not only do the spots act as a warning sign to possible attackers that they taste terrible, but they can secrete a fluid from joints in their legs, which gives them a foul taste.

### Studying bugs

Grab a magnifying glass or bug-viewing pot (with magnifying lid) and see if you can get up close to any of these micro superheroes. Can you spot anything that you hadn't seen before?

Why not design your own superbug? What does its costume look like? What would it smell like? What does it eat? What are its superpowers? Draw it in your nature journal (see page 108).

## Bees

A bee produces honey. It's a superpower for sure. They are the only insect that provides food for man. But it's hard work. Honey bees must gather nectar from two million flowers to make one pound of honey.

They can make music. The bees' buzz is the sound made by their wings, which beat about 11,400 times per minute.

A honey bee can fly for up to six miles, and as fast as 15mph (24kph).

The bee is a disco dancer. When a bee finds a source of nectar, it flies back to the hive to shows its friends and family where to find it. It does this by doing a dance, which positions the flower in relation to the sun and hive. This is called the 'waggle dance.' Totally amazing!

## Earth worms

They are indestructible! Well, sort of. If you cut a worm, depending on where the cut is, it can regenerate lost segments. The anterior (head) region is the most important part of a worm – if it remains intact, the worm can potentially survive, and may even grow a new tail. The lower fragment, however, once cut off from the rest of the worm, will simply die. (Please don't try this out; they prefer to be whole).

They have no nose or lungs but can still breathe air through their thin, permeable skin. This means that oxygen can pass through it. The moisture on a worm's skin helps to dissolve the oxygen. But, if a worm dries out, it will suffocate. So, if you see a worm sunbathing, perhaps find some moist soil so that it can breathe again.

Worms have been around for about 500 million years, even before dinosaurs!

## Ants

One of the world's strongest creatures in relation to its size, a single ant can carry 50 times its own body weight. If they can't lift something on their own, they'll work together to move bigger objects as a group.

Ants can send chemical signals, called pheromones, released through their body to send messages to other ants.

There are over 12,000 species of ants across the world. Funnily enough, they exist pretty much everywhere in the world (apart from ANTartica!).

# Know your trees

*Trees were once described to me as the lungs of the world and it's true, they give us oxygen, clean our air and give life to the world's wildlife. Some of them can grow to be giants and live for hundreds of years. Trees are vital and they don't just exist in parks, woodlands and mountains. You can find them lining our streets and roads, in car parks and around office blocks. In fact, one of the places they are most needed is in our cities and towns. Here are a few trees you might find in urban areas, see how many you can spot in your town.*

## Silver birch

*(Betula pendula)*

My daughter once told me that birch leaves look like stinging nettle leaves hanging on a tree, and I think she's right. They have whiteish bark, which sometimes looks like peeling tissue paper. They grow catkins in the late summer, which hang down like little caterpillars. Birch bark is excellent to use for fire lighting, making containers and boats. Their tolerance to poor soils and pollution make them ideal for cities.

### Tip
*The delicious sap of a silver birch tree can be drunk like a sweet juice.*

# London plane

*(Platanus x hispanica)*

The camouflage-style bark in olive green, brown and grey has a mottled mosaic-style pattern that make this tree stand out. Its large leaves are like a maple leaf or a five-pointed star. The unusual bark flakes off to shed pollutants that may be in the atmosphere: an amazing natural super power to deter nasty chemicals!

# Rowan

*(Sorbus aucuparia)*

The rowan tree, or mountain ash, is recognizable by its bright red berries and feathery leaves that grow in groups. Each one is long, oval and has jagged edges. Rowan berries are a great source of vitamin C. They have a sour taste and can be cooked to use in jams. These trees can survive for up to 200 years.

## Lime
*(Tilia cordata)*

The leaves are a beautiful bold heart shape and, if you gently touch one, you'll find they are a little hairy in the spring. Lime, or linden, trees grow sweet-smelling white flowers in the summer, but no limes I'm afraid! The leaves are delicious to eat fresh off the tree in early spring and the flowers can be made into a calming tea. Excellent for capturing carbon dioxide and reducing smog, they are perfect for urban spaces.

## Horse chestnut
*(Aesculus hippocastanum)*

This tree has large leaves that may remind you of a giant's green hands with its five (or sometimes more) fingers spanning out. It has rough, scaly, dark bark when mature. It is sometimes known as the 'sticky bud tree' due to its red, sticky buds. Horse chestnut is well known for bearing conkers (seeds) which are surrounded by a spiky green case, celebrated by children young and old for games, crafts or just the joy of collecting (see page 130 for activity ideas).

## English oak
*(Quercus robur)*

This tree supports more life than any other native tree species, in, around and under its wide shading canopy. An oak tree has distinctive round-lobed leaves with short stalks. In spring, it grows long, yellow hanging catkins, which distribute pollen into the air. After it has flowered, it will grow its recognizable nut, the acorn. Each fallen acorn is a potential new tree. An English oak tree can grow to 65–130ft (20–40m) tall and can then shorten itself in maturity in order to extend its life span. Very clever indeed.

# Why we need trees in our cities

- They help filter out pollution, sucking up harmful gases and chemicals that are polluting our environment and release clean oxygen for us to breathe.

- They absorb water using their amazing root systems, helping to prevent flooding.

- They provide shade, helping to cool our heat-producing cities.

- They can absorb noise.

- A single tree can be home to hundreds of insects, fungi, moss, mammals and plants. Without trees, many creatures like birds, bugs and squirrels would have nowhere to call home.

- They help to make our world look beautiful and they make us feel good by being around them.

# Plant power

*Some of our most common plants are dismissed as weeds and uprooted from people's gardens. But many of them have amazing properties that you may not know about. Not all plants like to grow in fields, woodlands, gardens or meadows. Some prefer the cracks of pavements, the shade of a graffiti wall, climbing up the side of a building or lining the side of a well-used road. So here I'm going to try and help dispel their bad reputation and give them the credit they deserve. I'm sure that once you start to recognize some of them, you'll start to see them everywhere.*

## Dandelion

### *(Taraxacum officinale)*

We may all think we know how to spot a dandelion by its beautiful yellow petals, its jagged green leaves and wish-granting puffy seed heads, but here are some more identification features to check for when out foraging.

### Identification features

Dandelions flower from around May to October. The deeply toothed leaves grow to around 2–10in (5–25cm) long but can be longer. The flower heads are yellow to orange coloured, and are open in the daytime but closed at night. The heads sit on a hollow stem. If you break a stem you will see a white, milky substance leak out of it. (Some people can have an allergic reaction after touching or eating this). The flower heads grow into round, fluffy seed heads. Each seed is attached to fine hairs, which enable the wind to spread them over long distances, like tiny parachutes.

### Amazing facts

One cup of raw dandelion greens is packed with vitamin A.

The common name dandelion comes from the French word *dent de lion*, meaning 'lion's tooth', referring to its jagged, tooth-like leaves.

The entire plant, including the leaves, stems, flowers and roots, is edible and nutritious, although I wouldn't recommend munching on the fluffy seed heads!

Dandelions are thought to have evolved about 30 million years ago.

A single seed can travel 5 miles (8km) before it finally reaches the ground.

## Daisy

*(Bellis perennis)*

The daisy will be familiar to most of us, rooted in the memory of many a childhood. I would sit for hours making daisy chains in my lunch break at school, just to bring home a wilted daisy crown for my mother to wear or a droopy bracelet for my sister. But did you know that the daisy has secrets?

### Identification features

Daisies bloom during the summer. They can grow from 3in–4ft (7.5cm–1.2m) in height, depending on the species and have edible green leaves. The flower consists of a large number of small flowers called florets, but don't assume all daisies are yellow and white. The colour depends on the species. Daisies can be red with a yellow centre, purple with a brown centre and many more combinations.

### Amazing facts

Daisies can be found on all continents except Antarctica.

There are around 4,000 species that differ in shape and colour.

Both the flowers and leaves are edible and are thought to have many medicinal uses. They are believed to slow bleeding, relieve indigestion, ease coughs and soothe aches and pains.

### Tip

*The name daisy is thought to come from the old English 'daes eag', which means 'day's eye', after the way it opens at dawn.*

### Tip

*Avoid picking garlic mustard in areas where pets are often walked or near busy roadsides.*

## Garlic mustard (Jack by the hedge, hedge garlic, poor man's mustard)

*(Alliaria petiolata)*

Garlic mustard adds a hint of garlic flavour to salads and other dishes. The clue as to where to find it is in one of its names – by the hedge. City and town foragers may find this slightly spicy plant nestled between tarmac and garden, or even in between supermarket fences. It often grows on waste ground. Due to where it grows, you need to be careful of where to pick it.

### Identification features

The larger leaves are heart shaped and the smaller ones (closer to the tip) are pointed, almost triangular. They smell like garlic when crushed between your fingers. The white flowers that come out around April to July are in leafless clusters, each with four petals in the shape of a cross. The flowers are also edible. The most flavoursome and tender leaves are the youngest ones at the top of the plant.

### Amazing facts

Garlic mustard can grow up to 6½ft (2m) tall.

It is one of the oldest spices used in Europe.

## Nettle
### *(Urtica dioica)*

Do not be put off by their stingy nature and invasive personalities. Nettles are amazing plants. They are medicinal, nutritious, and have even been used to clothe whole armies! So what do you really know about the nettle?

### Identification features

The soft, green leaves are 1–6in (2.5–15cm) long and grow on a green, wiry stem. The common nettle is best known for its needle-like stinging hairs that cover the heart-shaped leaves and stem. These stinging hairs act like hypodermic needles, injecting histamine and other chemicals into your skin upon contact. These chemicals are responsible for the burning, itchy sensation after touching the plant.

### Amazing facts

Nettles have been used to make clothing for 2,000 years. German army uniforms were almost all made from nettles during World War I, due to a shortage of cotton.

Nettles have been used to make green and yellow fabric dye.

They may hurt us, but nettles help their neighbours. They are good at protecting fellow plants by warding away fungal infections and diseases, keeping their patch healthy.

The spines of the stinging nettle contain chemicals called histamine and formic acid. When they touch tissue that is already in pain, it is said that these chemicals act as a counterirritant and actually help in reducing discomfort. Some people actually use the juice of the stinging nettle to treat nettle stings!

### Get to know a plant

Find one of these plants growing wild. Don't pick it; just look at it closely. Even use a magnifying glass if you have one. Examine its fine detail. Look for all the identification points.

Now write down your own description. Use your own words to try and describe the colour, its shapes, the textures. Now, while still looking at the plant, sketch it. Really try to make it look like the plant, include all of its fine detail. Go away from the plant and turn over the sketch so you can't see it. Try and draw it again, with all of its detail. See what you can remember. Look back at the picture. What did you remember? What did you forget?

Try this again and again with the same plant, until you feel you know it inside out. This is proven to be one of the best ways to get to know your plant world. Once you can draw it off by heart in all its glory, move on to another plant and get to know its friends.

# Blackberry
## (Rubus fruticosus)

We all know about blackberries. We have to wrestle a city of thorns to get to its delicious fruit, but it's worth it, right? But what do we actually know about it, apart from its sweet berry and thorny brambles?

## Identification features
The blackberry grows on a thorny shrub called a bramble bush. Brambles have long, thorny, arching shoots, which take root easily and can grow up to 3ft (2m) tall. They send up long, arching canes that produce the delicious blackberry fruit, which is ready to eat in late August/early September. The leaves are hairy, oval shaped and dark green with serrated edges. The pretty flowers are clusters of white or pink, which appear from late spring to early summer.

## Amazing facts
There are around 375 species of blackberry, which are found in almost all parts of the world. They are packed with vitamin C and the bramble vine can grow up to 3in (7.5cm) in a day!

**Tip**
*The bitter leaves of the plantain plant are edible and can be eaten cooked or raw.*

# Broadleaf plantain
## (Plantago major)

Plantain (not to be confused with the banana-shaped fruit) is a common weed that can most likely be found in your back garden, driveways, in bogs, along the edges of roads and footpaths, pretty much anywhere that the soil has ever been disturbed.

## Identification features
The leaves are green, egg-shaped and grow in a rosette with thick stems that meet at the base. When the stems are broken, they reveal stringy veins that remind me of the strings on a guitar. The flowers grow on a leafless stalk about the size and shape of a pencil. The seed head at the top looks like a tiny cat's tail.

## Amazing facts
The leaves have natural antibacterial and anti-inflammatory properties, making it great for soothing burns, reducing swelling and for treating bites or stings. In some cultures, plantain has been used to treat snake bites.

The genus name *Plantago* comes from the Greek word *planta*, which translates to mean 'footprint.' It is possible that as far back as the Stone Age, our prehistoric ancestors would have used plantain for medicine, eaten the leaves in stews and salads and ground the seeds to make a nutrient and protein-rich type of flour.

# Suburban surroundings

*by Tanya Taylor*

MY CITY SURROUNDINGS ARE A COUNCIL ESTATE, DEEP IN SUBURBIA. IT'S MADE UP OF ROW UPON ROW OF GREY TERRACED HOUSES, BLOCKS OF FLATS, CORNER SHOPS AND EVEN AN INTERNATIONAL AIRPORT. NEW VISITORS ARE OFTEN STARTLED BY THE THUNDEROUS ROAR OF AEROPLANES TAKING OFF, OR GLIDING IN, LOW OVER THE ROOFTOPS, TO LAND. SOMETIMES THEY'RE SO LOW, IT FEELS LIKE IF YOU JUMPED UP HIGH WITH YOUR ARMS STRETCHED OUT YOU COULD ALMOST TOUCH THEM.

When we were kids, my sister and I loved it in autumn when the big alder trees that lined our avenue shed their leaves, creating a sea of welcome colour in our suburban street. We'd jump and scrunch and roll around in the deep leaves. Sometimes we'd play 'chippy', serving each other portions of the leaves wrapped up expertly in newspaper, exactly as they did at the local fish'n'chip shop.

At the end of our road, the city stopped and gave way to the rolling countryside. Our school was surrounded by farmland and we were lucky to have a huge playing field. In spring, we'd sit in the warm sun and make daisy chains at lunchtime. When the grass had grown too lush, the big rumbling tractor would come and chop it all down and we'd make bird's nests and grass houses from the cuttings left behind. The muddy green grass stains wiped off easily from knees but refused to leave my white summer school dress. We loved the field and the escape it gave from the crowded classroom and hot tarmac playground.

Leading out of the grey estate were many footpaths to explore. They'd wind off into farmer's fields or down to the shore of the river where it merged with the sea. This estuary was, to us, a wetland paradise. Sometimes the tidal river would be high and rushing by, other times, not there at all. One time, my dad and I walked out across the dry riverbed to a boat stuck, stranded, left behind by the tide. We gave a little fright to the people inside when we boldly knocked on their door.

The far bank of the river was so far away that everything over there looked very small. A whole stretch of horizon made up with mini factories, with smoke swirling

*"At the end of our road, the city stopped and gave way to the rolling countryside."*

> *"We'd go walking and exploring for hours on end, learning about plants and birds, jumping ditches and playing hide-and-seek"*

from their chimneys. At night they'd look like magical fairy castles with twinkling lights sparkling out across the river.

My dad loved the suburban countryside and he wanted us to love it too. We'd go walking and exploring for hours on end, learning about plants and birds, jumping ditches and playing hide-and-seek in the long corn. Sometimes we'd even march along reciting our times tables, imprinting the information into our heads with every step. For an extra-special adventure, we'd go camping in the woods. If we got scared in the night, he'd tell us why we were safer there in the still shadows of the trees than in the bright lights of a big city.

# Town and city scavenger hunt

*It's easy to spot nature in parks or in your garden, but can you see it when you're walking around the cities and towns? Is it even there at all? I believe there's rarely a time when nature is not around us in one way or another; we may just have to open our eyes a little wider and look a little closer. Here is a scavenger hunt to help you do this.*

**AGE** Any
**TIME** Any
**TOOLS** A collecting bag if you want to take things home
**MATERIALS** List of things to find (see opposite page), a clipboard and a pen could be a good idea too

This absorbing activity can be done in small teams competing against each other, or just as part of a relaxed walk to encourage little ones to get outside and have an adventure.

Remember, you do not have to collect all the things on the list. Most of them are just about seeing them and ticking the box. Of course, there are a few things you could collect, and if you find a cool leaf on the ground and want to pop in it your nature journal (see page 108), go ahead. Just be mindful of not disturbing living things.

**Print with some of your findings when you get home**
If you decide to take home a few of the leaves and sticks you find, lay them out on a piece of paper, fill some spray bottles with a few drops of food colouring and water and spray over the top! See what cool patterns are made.

# Tick the box when you've found it

- [ ] Find something older than you
- [ ] Find something the same colour as your hair
- [ ] Find five of the same thing
- [ ] Spot a cloud that looks like an animal
- [ ] Find a building that nature has invaded
- [ ] Get within five paces of a bird
- [ ] Find something that crunches
- [ ] Find something prickly
- [ ] Find something that an animal might eat
- [ ] Find a flower with a smell
- [ ] Find a feather
- [ ] Find a tree with bark that is not brown
- [ ] Look for a flying insect
- [ ] See if you can find something living in a tree (big or small)
- [ ] Find something taller than you
- [ ] Find a seed or nut
- [ ] Look out for a new bud growing
- [ ] Find a patch of moss
- [ ] Look out for a spider's web (extra points if the spider is still weaving it!)
- [ ] Step on some tree roots
- [ ] Look out for a wild plant (something that's not been planted by a human)
- [ ] Find a stick as long as your arm

- [ ] Can you see grass growing through cracks in a pavement?
- [ ] Look at, but don't pick, a plant you could eat (look at our identification section on page 80)
- [ ] Try to spot an ant
- [ ] Spot a bird's nest
- [ ] Can you hear at least five different birdsongs?
- [ ] Find a sign of an animal having been in the area
- [ ] Find all the colours of the rainbow in different objects in nature (a red ladybird, an orange flower, a yellow leaf, green moss and so on)

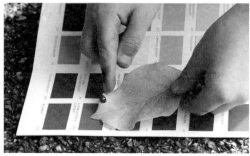

# Colour chart nature matching

**AGE** Any
**TIME** Any
**TOOLS** A colour chart card
**MATERIALS** None

*I love the simplicity of this activity. It can be done anywhere, for any length of time, in any weather with as many or as few people as you like. I've found that kids are amazed at how many more colours they can see when they look.*

You can go into most hardware and DIY shops and ask for a colour chart. They will most likely have many with lots of variations of one colour on one card. Take a few different ones so you have plenty of variety.

Now, with your colour charts, head out into the city or town and see what you can find that matches the colours on your chart. If you have a nature journal (see page 108) you could make a note of your colour matches in there.

### Things to think about
• What colours do you expect to see in nature?
• What colours do you expect to see in towns and cities?
• Can you find all the colours on your charts?
• Are they all natural?
• Which colours are easy to find?
• Which colours are hard to find?

### Tip
*There are lots of places where you can look to match your colour chart: graffiti on walls, parks or pavements, planted flower beds, trees sporting berries and bustling city markets, for example.*

# A night walk

*Have you ever gone out at night just to find out what you can see and hear? Maybe you've heard a bark or a snuffle, or perhaps a hoot? But it might not be quite what you think. Did you know that deer can bark? Did you know that foxes can make a sound like a cough? Did you know that not only do owls hoot, but some owls screech? Why not venture out and investigate the noises and sights of the night for yourself?*

**AGE** 7+ (with adult supervision)
**TIME** Any (but I would recommend 1 hour+)
**TOOLS** See box below of things to take

Before you head out, make a plan, ask an adult to accompany you and pack a bag with useful kit to make sure you are equipped for your adventure. Then wait for dusk to fall.

## Things you might see and hear

### Hedgehogs

Go into your garden or to your local green space on a summer's night. Hedgehogs like to hide under garden sheds, near compost heaps or in hedges. The most obvious signs are footprints. Hedgehog prints are about 1in (2.5cm) long and very slightly longer than this in width. The front toes are quite widely splayed, but the back toes are long and thin. Their poo is about $1/2$–2in (1.5–5cm) long and $3/8$in (1cm) in diameter and quite dark coloured. Hedgehogs are noisier than you might think. You may hear them snuffling and huffing around as they search for food. In the spring they can get very noisy as they fight over females.

## What to take with you

- A head torch. Keep it switched off when trying to spot animals, but a good head torch with fresh batteries will help guide your way. It is also a good idea to keep it switched on while you are near a road, as this will make sure you can be seen.
- Wear a high visibility jacket. This will make sure you are easy to spot by each other and by any road users nearby. If you are concerned about showing up, take it off when you are stationary in a 'hide' spot.
- Wear warm, weatherproof clothing, especially if you're keeping still for any length of time.
- Wear boots. They give a better grip than shoes on uneven ground, when you can't always see your footing clearly.
- A fully charged mobile phone with stored emergency numbers.
- A bag, in case you find anything interesting and to store waterproofs in, if necessary.
- A camera.
- A pair of binoculars so that you can get up close and personal without scaring anything off.
- A notebook to record all of your findings.

## Bats

Bats are easiest to spot in the summer months when they are out hunting insects. Choose a dark area with no street lamps, just before sunset. Bats particularly like to be by water so canals and rivers are a good place to try. Dry, still nights are best as they need to use less energy to hunt in these conditions. Standing on a bridge can be an effective place for a good view as you can see the water in both directions, or find a straight part of the waterway so that you can see as far as possible. Bats often feed in sheltered areas too, where swarms of flying insects gather. It's impressive to watch them hunt in the sky.

## Tip

*Look out for any local nature groups running bat-spotting walks that you could take part in.*

## Foxes

Most foxes are shy and secretive, so think about getting away from really noisy areas. Dusk is best. Cemeteries can be a great place to see foxes, as well as parks. But they don't just hang out in green areas: foxes can often be seen in town, busily foraging out in the streets, or even in industrial estates if waste has been left behind. Although foxes are mostly silent animals, they have a broad repertoire of sounds. They have over a dozen screeches, barks, cough-like sounds, grunts and growls, from a cub's small barks for its mother's attention, to warning calls, barks and screams to locate another fox, scare off a predator or attract a mate.

## Cats

Cats are not actually nocturnal, but can often be found exploring the streets at night-time, fighting, hunting and howling to one another across the streets. Just because they are not wild animals, it doesn't make them less interesting to observe and listen to. Plus, you may not need to go very far to see or hear one. They are naturally most active at dusk and dawn and sometimes make loud noises calling out to other cats or crying because they're bored!

## Badgers

Badger watching can be exciting, like witnessing a wild theatre show! Badgers have often been spotted in urban areas, crossing roads and looking for food in people's gardens.

Their eyesight is not brilliant but their sense of smell and hearing are amazing. When looking for badgers, go out at dusk, but think about the sound your waterproof clothing makes when you move. Don't use soap or anything perfumed before you go out either. They will sense danger and leave immediately, as the chances are they will smell or hear you before you see them. If you do get lucky one evening, and if you're super-quiet and patient, you might just see one of these charismatic animals playing, grooming or feeding. The best time to look for them is during June and July.

## Owls

For owl watching, wear dark, quiet clothing (think about the sound of your clothing as you move). If you want to use binoculars, use lightweight ones, which are effective in low light. Keep your distance from a nest or roost sites. It's best to arrive at your watching site before dark, and remain hidden. Each species of owl has a different call, from high-pitched screeches to hoots. It's the tawny owl that makes the familiar twit-twoo sound. Yet, did

you know that this call is made by both a male and female calling to each other? The female makes a 'ke-wick', and the male answers with something like 'hoo-hoo-oo'. Owl hoots and screeches might be to claim a particular territory, warning other owls to stay away or might be a way to attract a mate.

## The Moon

Whether in the city, the town or the countryside, anywhere in the world, we are all looking at the same bright, glowing moon. But the Moon itself doesn't actually emit any light. What we see when we look at the Moon is sunlight reflected off its surface. It is easy to study the Moon with a pair of binoculars. If you stay away from bright street lights and make sure you have a clear line of sight, with no trees in the way, you should be able to get a good look at it.

## The stars

Although the stars that we see in the sky don't differ depending on whether we are in a town, the city or countryside, what we see when we look up will change, depending on the amount of light pollution in the area. There are ways to stargaze in an urban setting. Choose a clear, cloudless evening. Winter evenings tend to be better as summer heat can create humidity and haze. The trick to stargazing is to find the biggest bit of sky you can. Do you have access to a loft window or a rooftop, perhaps? What about looking out the windows of upper-storey flats, or maybe just a local park? These places, especially when on the outskirts of a city, can all work well as star-gazing spots.

# More ideas for nocturnal wildlife watching

When the sun goes in and night falls, many creatures are only just getting ready to start their routines: eating, hunting, digging, protecting their homes, attracting mates and for some, trying not to get eaten! This is because they are nocturnal: creatures of the night. Some use the dark as a cover for hunting, others use the shadows as a cloak for hiding. Here are some ways in which you might be able to gather some clues as to what is out there lurking, hiding or stalking through the night.

- **Make a track trap, see page 58** This is a great way to observe which animals have been around during the night while you are snug in your bed.

- **Invest in an infrared, water-resistant trail/wildlife camera** Buy one with night vision and you may just capture some rare night-time insights into the goings on in your garden or near your house. I recommend only leaving the camera unattended on your own property.

- **Set up a hidden viewing area** You can do this in your garden or in a park near your house. Make sure you have a responsible adult with you.

- **Leave some food and water out for wildlife** Do this if you have a garden, and have permission to do so. Constantly putting out food can make wild mammals reliant on your source of unnatural food, but putting out a bit of food every now and again during winter allows them to top up any low stocks and gives them a helping hand through the cold and harsh weather. Put out fresh food at dusk and don't forget a dish of fresh water. Hedgehogs like cat food (fresh each time); badgers like fruits and nuts, root vegetables and cooked potatoes.

- **Bird-box webcam** My family and I got a lot of joy out of one of these cameras. You put them into your bird box and the camera connects to your television, letting you see into an ordinarily private world. We got to see a family of blue tits make their nest, lay eggs, hatch, grow and fledge. We also got to witness some of the harsh realities of nature when we saw a magpie take one of the baby birds. Although sad at times, it was also incredibly educational and a blessing to be able to observe.

- **Most moths fly at night** You can watch for them in your garden, or any green space. Choose a cloudy and still night, as moths are not fans of flying in the wind. Try shining a torch light. Many moths are attracted to bright lights. A fun way to see them is to hang a white sheet over a clothesline or bush, shine a torch on it and wait for them to arrive.

# Home crafts

CRAFTING IS UP THERE AS ONE OF MY FAVOURITE
PASTIMES. THE IDEA OF USING NATURAL MATERIALS TO
CRAFT WITH REALLY APPEALS TO ME. IT'S CHEAP, OFTEN
WITHOUT ANY COST AT ALL, AND REDUCES THE RISK OF
WASTE, AS WELL AS CREATING SOMETHING THAT CAN
ULTIMATELY EITHER BE COMPOSTED OR RECYCLED. HERE
ARE A FEW IDEAS TO DO IN YOUR KITCHEN AT HOME,
PLAYING WITH NATURE WHATEVER THE WEATHER.

# Felted soap dinky

*This is a fantastic little craft project that all ages can get involved with. Not only are they fun to make, but are also lovely to use in the bath or shower. In their felted shell, they last a lot longer than an uncovered bar of soap and are an eco-friendly alternative to soaps and shampoos in plastic bottles. For this project you will need to obtain wool fleece. You can buy this cleaned, even dyed in lovely colours, online or in some craft shops, or use Merino wool tops.*

**AGE** 2+
**TIME** 40 minutes
**TOOLS** Scissors
**MATERIALS** About ¹/₁₆oz (5g) of clean wool fleece (dyed or natural) or Merino wool tops, a bar of soap, washing-up liquid, old tights (use the foot ends only, cut to about 12in/30cm in length), spray bottle, bucket of water

## Tip
*Although this project is a simple one, it is also a wet one! Choose a suitable work surface that will tolerate water such as a kitchen worktop, sink draining board or, even better, outside.*

### Step 1
Divide the wool into short lengths, approximately double the length of your soap. Tease the wool apart with your fingers until you can just see the soap through it. Layer up the flattened and teased-apart pieces of wool over the soap. Repeat this step several times but lay each piece of wool in a criss-cross fashion, until the bar of soap is completely covered on one side. It's important not to make the layers too thick.

### Step 2
When one side is covered it is now time to make this layer wet. Half fill the water spray bottle with hot water and add a small dash of washing-up liquid but do not shake the bottle as you don't want it to be foamy. Use your spray bottle to saturate the wool.

### Step 3
Carefully press the wet layers down so that it all comes together, folding the edges over to the other side. Repeat steps 1–3 twice more. By the end of this process you should have at least two layers on each side. If you want a super-thick soap dinky you can add more layers if you wish.

### Step 4
Once your soap is completely covered, back and front, it is time to carefully put this into your section of tights, folding any excess over. This will make sure your soap is securely inside and won't spontaneously pop out.

### Step 5
Spray with more water and soap mixture and gently rub, first one side, using a circular motion, and then the other. Once you have done this a few times, you can rub a bit more vigorously, a bit like you are washing your hands with it, and then squeeze. You don't want it to hold lots of water and swell. This is the felting process. By gently rubbing, you are encouraging the wool fibres to bind together. The hotter the water you use, the quicker the wool will felt and the more time you spend rubbing, the firmer your felt will be. Adding more soap and warm water will help the process.

### Step 6
Every 5–10 minutes you will need to carefully take your soap out of your tights to make sure that it is not felting together with them. You can use this opportunity to check how well your soap is felting. To do this, run your fingertips gently across the top of the wool. If your fibres move, you need to felt more, so return to your tights. If it holds tightly and does not move around, your felting is complete. Discard the tights to use again next time. Rinse all the washing-up liquid from it by running it under a tap or by dunking in a bucket of water. Now leave to dry and use it whenever you need a wash!

**Tip**
*The felt shrinks with the soap as you use it, so at the end you'll have a very handy 'scrubby' to use for cleaning.*

**AGE** 7+ (with supervision for steaming)
**TIME** 2 hours+
**TOOLS** Saucepan, a large smoothish stick or dowel rod, extra-small sticks, a rod or chopsticks to prop up your bundle in the saucepan
**MATERIALS** Fabric to print on to (100% cotton or white silk chiffon works well), various collected fresh leaves, water, string, iron modifier (optional, instructions below)

*Tip*
*I used a ready-made 100% cotton tote bag to print on.*

# Eco leaf printing

*This method of printing on to fabric is an effective way to capture nature's beautiful patterns. You can adapt and tweak the instructions, experimenting endlessly with new materials and patterns.*

## Variation

Using natural dyes can be hit and miss. Some plants and trees need a little more help to bring out and fix their colour, which is when you might use a mordant. A mordant sticks to the fibres of the fabric and dye sticks to the mordant, creating a chemical bond. Using an iron modifier can make these leaf prints stronger and bolder. Wearing gloves to protect your hands, dip the leaves into the iron modifier before laying them on the fabric. You can also dip the fabric, if you like. The rest of the process is the same as the steps above.

**To make an iron modifier**
Gather up a bunch of rusty nails, screws, washers, nuts and bolts. Fill a jar with 1 part white vinegar and 2 parts water. Add the rusty items. Lightly close the jar with the lid (don't screw it on very tight). Let it sit for about 1–2 weeks. Strain off the liquid when you want to use it.

### Step 1
Make the fabric wet by running it under a tap and wringing it out. Lay the fabric out flat. Arrange your collected fresh leaves on to half of the fabric (it helps if the fabric is rectangular). When you are happy with the design, fold over the other half of the fabric over the leaves, covering them up.

### Step 2
Place the dowel or stick on to one end of the folded fabric and roll the fabric very tightly around it to make a sausage.

### Step 3
Next, wrap string around the sausage very tightly, to make sure there is good contact between the fabric and the leaves for the printing to work.

### Step 4
This is where adult supervision is necessary. As you are going to steam the bag above the water, add your extra dowel rod or chopstick to the saucepan first to prop up your sausage so it will remain out of the boiling water. Now add your sausage and pour in your water, enough to cover the bottom of the pan (it's fine if it touches the sausage, but it shouldn't cover it).

### Step 5
Heat the saucepan on the hob, bringing the water to a boil. Place a lid on top to keep in the steam, and continue gently simmering for an hour or two. Check it every 10 minutes or so, to make sure the water doesn't boil dry; add more water as needed.

### Step 6
Carefully take the bundle out of the water and let it cool completely. Leave it to set overnight. The longer the better, if you have the patience! Cut off the string and unroll the fabric, remove the leaves and allow it to dry.

# Leaf watercolour printing

*The best thing about this activity is all the ways in which you can use your art afterwards. Bookmarks, book covers, cut into bunting, wrapping paper: you could even put it in a frame just as it is. Remember, you do not have to be a great artist to create beautiful pieces of art. Here, Nature has done all the hard work for you.*

**AGE** 7+

**TIME** 30 minutes (not including leaf collection or paint-drying time)

**TOOLS** Paintbrush or sponges

**MATERIALS** Watercolour paints, good-quality paper (we used a roll of lining wallpaper), freshly picked leaves, a cup of water

## Step 1

First choose your leaves. You want them to be fresh so they don't break apart on the picture. Ferns and maples are good to experiment with as they have great details and shape. Once your leaves are chosen, create a water wash in which to lay the leaves on. Take a clean brush and paint your paper with water. You can experiment with this. Paint the entire paper all over or just add splodges, it's up to you.

## Step 2

For the background, don't make your colour choices too dark – mix with white watercolour to help lighten them up. This bit needs to be done quickly so that the paper and paint stay wet. Make splotches of colours, drips, grand flourishes; any way to quickly get lots of pigment on to your paper will do. Don't try too hard here. It's all about spontaneous strokes.

1

2

3

4

5

### Step 3

While the paint is still very wet, lay the leaves down on the paper. The leaves may overlap or even go off the page. You could tear some, lay some upside down. Just go for it. You just want to make sure that they stick down firmly and stay put.

### Step 4

Once the leaves are down, you'll need to add some more colour. You can dilute the paint with water or use undiluted, whichever you like. Load your brush or sponge with colour and add to the paper, filling in the gaps of the leaves wherever you can see the paper. You can add brush strokes or just patches, but be careful that the leaves don't move. Add more in places you want to emphasize with extra colour or places that look as if they may be too dry for the leaves to stick down.

### Step 5

The leaves must stay on the paper until it is completely dry in order to capture all of their fine details. Be patient. Waiting will pay off, so leaving them overnight is best. Once dry, carefully remove the leaves.

### Variation for pre-schoolers

Why not try doing leaf prints with washable markers? Just dampen the paper with moist kitchen towel. Draw on the back of the leaves with the washable makers, but carefully enough so that the leaves don't rip. You can mix colours if you like. Then press down on to the paper. If your paper dries out too quickly, just gently wipe it over again with your damp kitchen towel. This makes great wrapping paper once dry.

# Pine-cone deer

*This is a wonderful way to give a pine cone a whole new lease of life. Autumn is a great time to collect fallen pine cones and I love using foraged natural materials in crafts, seeing all the fun ways they can be turned into something new. These little deer have lovely characters (then again, add googly eyes to anything and it makes me smile). You can use them as festive tree decorations if you like, or hang them anywhere at any time of year.*

**AGE** 3+
**TIME** 20 minutes+
**TOOLS** Scissors, glue gun
**MATERIALS** Pine cones, sticks, googly eyes, little red craft pompoms (or small balls of screwed-up tissue paper or red paper), brown felt or cardboard, ribbon or twine for hanging, permanent black marker pen

## Safety warning
Adult supervision needed for using a glue gun.

## Step 1
Collect your pine cones. With the pointy end facing down, glue two little sticks on the other end to make its antlers.

## Step 2
Glue on the googly eyes.

## Step 3
Draw two small teardrop shapes on to the brown felt or cardboard with a marker pen, for the ears, and cut them out. Glue these on to the side of the head at the top.

## Step 4
Glue on the red nose at the tip of the pine cone (or wherever you would like his nose to be). If you want to hang up your deer, glue on a loop of ribbon or twine at the top.

1

2

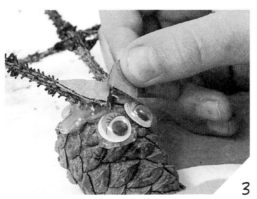

3

4

# Measuring stick

*When you are out and about, you may find a track, a hole in something or perhaps an extra-large leaf. You might want to look it up in an identification book when you get home, especially if it's something that can't be collected up, like an animal track or a hole in a tree. By placing your measuring stick next to your object of interest and taking a photo, it will help to give it some perspective to refer back to later. Trust me: it'll become a valuable part of your kit as well as helping to back up cool stories to your friends later about how 'that thing' was especially huge or the teeny tiniest thing you ever saw!*

**AGE** Any
**TIME** 10 minutes+
**TOOLS** Ruler, paintbrush, secateurs
**MATERIALS** Sturdy stick 12in (30cm) long (it must be exact), black permanent marker pen and coloured ones or acrylic paints

## Tip
*When searching for suitable sticks to use, make a game of who can find one the closest to 12in (30cm) long just by estimating, no measuring!*

1

2

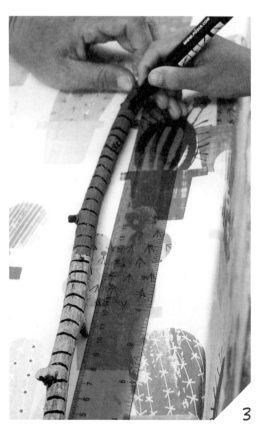

3

## Step 1
First you need to find a suitable stick. Make sure it isn't too flimsy and thin or too thick and heavy. Ask a grown-up to help you cut it exactly to 12in (30cm) long with some secateurs.

## Step 2
You could peel off the bark, perhaps rub the edges on hard ground to make them smooth, or just leave it as it is. Then paint or draw on it for decoration using acrylic paints or marker pens. Go rainbow coloured, paint it in camouflage colours, paint it all red with black spots – whatever your heart desires.

## Step 3
For the next bit, you must be exact. Carefully, using the ruler and black marker pen so that it shows up, draw lines to mark out inches and centimetres until you get all the way to the end. Now your measuring stick is finished and ready to use.

# Beeswax wraps

*Although this activity is not strictly within the boundaries of 'Forest School', I believe it has a place in this book. Overuse of plastic in the modern world has many negative impacts upon our planet. Here is a fun activity to make a plastic-free alternative to cling film. You can make them using your favourite coloured and patterned cotton fabrics to brighten up your lunch box. Wrap up your sandwiches in them and help save the planet at the same time!*

**AGE** 5+ (with assistance during the heating stages)
**TIME** 1 hour
**TOOLS**
Double-boiler pan or a glass bowl set in a saucepan, oven, large baking sheet, two thick paintbrushes (they will not be able to be used for paint again afterwards, so use an old one that you don't mind dedicating to the purpose)
**MATERIALS** Three or four 12 x 12in (30 x 30cm) squares of thick cotton fabric (organic if possible), $^1/_4$oz (7g) sustainably sourced pine resin, 1$^1/_4$oz (35g) beeswax pastilles or grated beeswax, $^1/_2$tbsp organic jojoba oil, wooden lolly stick or other compostable stirrer, greaseproof paper

## Step 1

Preheat the oven to 300°F (150°C). Place the pine resin, beeswax and jojoba oil into a double-boiler pan (or a glass bowl set into a saucepan). Add water to the bottom of the saucepan so that the mixture inside the double boiler or glass bowl is below the waterline. Turn the hob on to a medium-high heat. Allow the ingredients to melt and mix together, stirring occasionally with the lolly stick. This should take about 15 to 20 minutes.

## Step 2

Cover a large metal baking sheet with greaseproof paper. It should be larger than your biggest piece of fabric. Spread one of your pieces of fabric flat on to the greaseproof paper. Using the paintbrush, brush the melted mixture lightly over the fabric. It might solidify in places, but you will be able to redistribute it later. Remember, it's easier to add more later than to take the excess away now.

## Step 3

Place the baking sheet, greaseproof paper and coated fabric into the oven for about two minutes. Remove it from the oven and look for any dry spots of fabric that are not covered in wax. Brush the mixture over these uncovered areas, applying more coating as needed. If you notice any uneven areas after adding more mixture, you can place it back into the oven for a few minutes to smooth out.

## Step 4

Place the next piece of dry fabric on top of the coated fabric you have just made, to soak up any excess mixture. Hang up the completed wrap to dry and then repeat steps 2 and 3 for the new piece and any remaining ones. Work quickly, as you don't want the wax to solidify, but be very careful as the tray will be hot from the oven. Drying only takes a few minutes. Repeat with additional pieces of fabric until you have run out of your beeswax mixture.

### Doing our bit
We have a responsibility, both young people and old, to protect our Earth, to learn to be more sustainable, to live a little lighter and, although it may not be possible to do all of this all of the time, we can all do our little bit.

1

2

3

4

## Using the beeswax wraps

Depending on how often you use them, you will need to refresh the wraps every 6–12 months. Simply pop them back in the oven for a couple of minutes, remove, then brush a light coat of the melted resin, wax and oil mixture evenly over the cloth.

They are easy to keep clean. Wash them in cool water with a mild soap and air dry. Store them folded up in a drawer, away from sunlight and heat sources.

The heat from your hands should help to mould the fabric around your bowls, containers or sandwiches for your picnic.

You can use them to cover or wrap up pretty much anything, as the ingredients in them mean that they are food safe and they even contain anti-bacterial ingredients. However, they are NOT recommended for using on or around meat or fish products.

# Nature journal

*A nature journal is great to take out and about with you wherever you go. Use it to record animal tracks you might find, draw a picture of the clouds you saw or tuck interesting leaves in to draw or print with later. You could use it to write about your adventures, fact or fiction! You could stick in photos of your interactive botanical art, your shadow drawings, or your recipes. Whatever you use it for, fill it with love and creativity.*

**AGE** 7+

**TIME** 1 hour

**TOOLS** Ruler, sharp fabric scissors

**MATERIALS** Spray adhesive (you can substitute with PVA glue but it is not as easy to use), thick card for the cover (you can use an old hardback book cover that you don't need any more, thick card or mount board – we used an empty cereal box), two pieces of fabric large enough to cover the size of book you want to make (with some extra allowance at the edges), a minimum of five extra-large thick elastic bands, paper and card to create your pages in assorted sizes, colours and shapes

## Step 1

Cut three pieces of thick card: a front and a back that are the same size and a narrower piece for the spine. The sizes are up to you. The spine will be the thickness of the journal so make this at least 1in (2.5cm) wide so that the journal has room to bulge a little when stuffed with treasures. There's really no limit on how wide you can go but you will need to check that your elastic bands are big enough to go around the spine without making it bend. You could reinforce this bit with an extra layer of card to make it thicker and stronger.

Lay out the piece of fabric that you would like to use for the outside cover, with the right side (the one you want to see) facing down. Place the three pieces of card on top of the fabric, in the centre, with all three pieces lined up next to one another. Leave about a 1in (2.5cm) gap all the way around the edge to fold over later. Leave a ¼in (6mm) gap between the spine and the front and back covers to create a hinge. Using the spray adhesive, cover each piece of card and fix back into place on the fabric.

### Patterned fabric

Why not print a leaf pattern on to your fabric before you start? We used fabric paint (but you could also use acrylic paints), sponges and paintbrushes to dab paint around the edges of different-shaped leaves.

## Step 2

Trim the second piece of fabric to the exact overall size of the pieces of card when they are placed together. Spray all over the pieces of card with the adhesive and then glue the second piece of fabric on to them, with the right side facing outwards. The card should now be hidden.

## Step 3

Fold over the excess fabric on the top, bottom and sides and stick it down using the spray adhesive to keep it in place. This dries pretty quickly, but make sure it is completely dry before moving on to the next step.

## Step 4

While the cover is drying, it's time to prepare your inside pages to create 'signatures'. A signature is simply a group of papers that are folded together. Each piece of paper you use in this journal will be folded in half. It can be helpful to find and cut your papers to a similar size to your book cover, but feel free to mix and match different sizes and shapes to your liking. You can use old cards, old letters, posters, even nature identification sheets.

Once you have all the papers folded, group them into sets of six pages or more. You'll want a total of 5–7 groups of folded papers.

## Tip

*To fold the papers, it is helpful to use a ruler to press down on the folds. A nice clean fold will give you better results.*

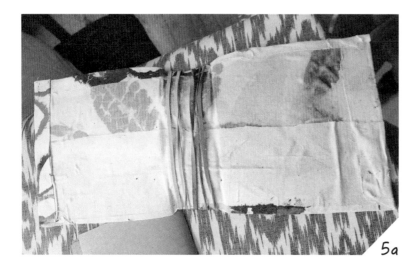

5a

5b

**Tip**

*Why not stick in a few envelopes using the spray adhesive? That way you'll have a nifty way to store some of your treasures.*

6

**Step 5**

Take the elastic bands and wrap them over the spine of the book. If it bends a little bit, don't worry, it will straighten up once the signatures are in. If it bends a lot, then you will need to find bigger elastic bands.

**Step 6**

Insert the signatures between the elastic bands one at a time. Make sure each signature has its own elastic band. Each time you add a signature, turn these pages to the left before you add another group. You'll find it comes together quickly and easily. If you don't like where something is, it's very easy to slide out any piece of paper and move it around.

## Ideas for filling your journal

Some people find an empty journal daunting and don't know how to begin or how to fill the pages, so here are a few prompts to get you started.

• Draw something you see using a charcoal pencil.

• Write a story about an animal you have seen, pretending that you are that animal.

• Sketch a bug you can see and write what you think its superpower could be.

• Describe something you can smell while out and about.

• Draw a picture of something smaller than you and something bigger than you.

• Describe the sounds you have heard while out – can you identify any of them?

• Find a flower and write a fact file on it, focusing on any tiny details.

• Draw a picture of the sky today. What clouds can you see?

• Draw a picture of a tree and take a bark rubbing to go with it.

• What birds can you see? Can you describe their song?

• Write about the ground you are walking on using three descriptive words.

• Write down all the colours that you've seen on your walk today and where you found them. Try to recreate them at home with paint, crayons or pens.

• Describe the light outside today. Has it changed at all?

• Does the air have a smell?

# Leaf bunting

**AGE** Any
**TIME** 20 minutes+
**TOOLS** Craft hole punch in various shapes (or an office-style circular hole punch will do), glue gun
**MATERIALS** A selection of leaves (fresh and waxy ones like rhododendron work best, but any will work fine), a length of ribbon (depending on how long you want your bunting to be)

*This activity is super simple, yet really effective. The bunting catches the light really nicely when hung in windows and lasts a surprising amount of time when you use fresh leaves. It is also easy enough for really young children to join in.*

### Step 1

Go out for a walk and collect your leaves. About 10 is a good number. If it's not a tree from your own garden, make sure you are respectful and do not take too many from one tree and ask permission if the tree is on someone's private property.

### Step 2

Using your hole punch, make patterns in the leaves. Cut as many shapes into them as you like, but make sure you leave some leaf still connected in between each hole.

### Step 3

Decide where you want each leaf to sit along your ribbon and glue them into place using the glue gun, with the help of an adult. Alternatively, you can thread your leaves on using the holes that you punched. Now hang up and enjoy.

### Tip

You could also paint your leaves with acrylic paints. If you use a piece of paper underneath to protect your table, you'll find you make interesting designs under the leaves too.

1

2a

2b

3a

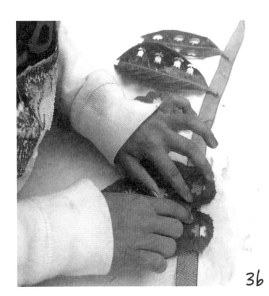

3b

# Planting and using herbs

*I love growing plants with my children. They relish the whole process: planting the seeds, and nurturing them to grow with water, even stories and songs! And then picking and, of course, eating the edible ones. You don't even have to have a garden to do this. Herbs are a perfect thing to grow inside. Plus, in my opinion, herbs are amazing. You can use them in cooking, in salads, in teas and medicines and some of them can make delicious refreshing cool drinks on a hot day. Young children may need a little help with sewing the initial pouches, but the planting (and eating) bit can be enjoyed by all.*

**AGE** 2+ (for planting); 7+ (for sewing and creating the pots)
**TIME** 1 hour
**TOOLS** Sharp fabric scissors, sewing needle
**MATERIALS** Herb seeds, compost, empty plastic water/drink bottle, a pair of old jeans, extra-strong polyester thread, letter stamps and fabric scraps for labelling (optional)

### Step 1
Cut the bottom section off the empty plastic bottle, at the height you would like your plant pot to be.

### Step 2
Place the plastic pot on to the bottom part of a jeans leg and cut it off, leaving an extra 1in (2.5cm) of fabric to spare.

### Step 3
Turn the cut jeans leg inside out and stitch along the bottom, cutting off the corners to make a small rounded pouch. Your sewing does not have to be neat here – a simple running stitch (in and out) will work just brilliantly.

### Step 4
Cut a belt loop off the jeans and stitch it securely to the top of the jeans-leg pouch in the middle, while they are still inside out. Secure it in place with a few stitches by going over and over again. Just a simple running stitch is fine.

### Step 5
Turn the pouch the right way round and write your labels. You can stamp out the names of the plant on to scrap fabric strips and glue them on with a glue gun, or you can write the labels with acrylic paint pens. We wrote our plant names in Latin.

### Step 6
Now pot up your seeds into the plastic pots and pop them into their little pouches and watch them grow.

### Step 7
We used an old plank of wood and hammered in some nails to hang our pouches up but you can just leave them sitting on a windowsill.

### Simple ways to use herbs
- Use mint in hot or cold water with a slice of lemon for a delicious and calming drink.
- Chop up basil really fine and freeze in ice-cube trays. Add to a pizza or pasta sauce.
- Thyme is fantastic for soothing sore throats. Add to hot water with honey for a lovely drink.
- Lavender ice cubes are amazing when added to water and lemon on a hot day.

### Did you know?
There is only one correct Latin name for any plant species whereas there can be hundreds of common names for the same plant.

1

2

3

4

5

6

7

# Berries in your boots

*You certainly don't need a garden to grow these and who doesn't enjoy a juicy ripe strawberry? All you need is a pair of old wellington boots that don't fit or have holes in and an outdoor space like a front porch, a driveway, a balcony or back doorstep – anywhere that can get sunlight. Try this in late spring.*

**AGE** 3+ (with supervision for cutting)
**TIME** 40 minutes
**TOOLS** Old wellington boots, craft knife, watering can with water
**MATERIALS** Gravel, 6 strawberry plants, soil, eggshells, petroleum jelly

### Tip
You can grow all sorts of other plants in old wellies, not just strawberries. Try herbs, tomatoes, spinach, even carrots!

### Step 1
With adult supervision, cut a hole in each side of each boot, about 2in (5cm) in diameter. Cut another hole the same size about halfway up on the opposite side. Fill the bottom of each boot with gravel. This will provide the plants with drainage. It needs to be about 1in (2.5cm) deep.

### Step 2
Add your soil up to the first hole. Plant your first strawberry plant, feeding the plant through the hole. Press down firmly on the soil. Add more soil up to the second hole and add another plant in the same way. Fill again with soil all the way to the top and plant another one coming out of the top, covering the roots with soil and pressing down. Do this with both of your welly boots. Water well.

### Step 3
Cover any bare soil with broken eggshells and smear the petroleum jelly around the top. This will help protect your berries from the local slugs and snails. Water regularly. You can choose to feed them with tomato feed once a week for a better chance of growing healthy strawberries. As long as they can be in the sun and get watered daily, you should have delicious strawberries in about two months.

# Sack of potatoes

*The wonderful thing about this activity is that you do not need an outdoor space to be able to grow vegetables. You can grow potatoes in a bin bag with drainage holes and be eating roasties 90 days later!*

**AGE** Any
**TIME** 20 minutes
**TOOLS** Scissors, trowel, watering can with water
**MATERIALS** Seed potatoes (chitted), bin bag, hessian or burlap sack (try garden centres or hardware shops for this), potting compost

### Chitting potatoes

You'll need to chit your potatoes first, which means they have started producing shoots. It's easy to do. All you need to do is put some potatoes in an old egg box, leave them somewhere they can get plenty of light and wait until they start to sprout. Start chitting from late January and about six weeks before you intend to plant out the potatoes. The potatoes are ready to be planted out when the shoots are about ½–1in (1.5–2.5cm) long.

### Step 1

Make some holes in the bottom of your bin bag. This is so that the water can drain out and your plants don't get too wet. Make about 8–10 holes using your scissors.

### Step 2

Place your bag inside your hessian or burlap sack. Fill the bin bag a quarter full with compost. Roll down the sides of the bag to soil level. Add three potatoes, eyes up (this means make sure the majority of the sprouts are facing upwards). Cover thinly with compost and water.

### Step 3

Water whenever the soil looks dry. As they grow, cover the shoots with the compost once a month for three months, rolling up the sides of the bin bag as the compost levels rise. After about 90 days, you can split the side of the bin bag open with a knife or scissors or dig down (like a potato lucky dip) and see what you can find.

# Stick boats

*This simple activity combines crafts with exploration. You can make these little sail boats from 100% natural and foraged materials. With just a couple of simple steps, you'll soon be sailing the high seas or at least a few puddles, streams or even your kitchen sink if you want to test drive them first!*

From your foraged materials, find yourself a base for your boat. A flattish piece of bark or light piece of wood works well. Now find a sail. A leaf works beautifully. Use the cocktail stick to fix the sail on to the base by carefully passing it through the leaf at the top and bottom and then pressing it down into the bark to secure in place. Now set sail for the high seas, or at least a bucket of tap water!

**AGE** 2+

**TIME** 5 minutes+

**MATERIALS** Foraged materials like bark, leaves, flowers etc., cocktail sticks, paddling pool/sink/bucket (or stream if you have access), paper straws for racing

URBAN FOREST SCHOOL

## More ideas
- Try using grass to weave around the base of the boat, or use flowers as sails.
- Have a boat race with a friend using straws to blow wind into the sails of the boats to propel them along.
- Remember, masts and sails don't necessarily make them go faster in a race, it just means you can see them for longer as they drift away so make them big and bold if you can!
- Can you find enough feathers to make a beautiful sail from them?
- Try tying up a bundle of sticks to make a buoyant base.

**Tip**
*You can make these without the foam, making them easily recyclable. But using foam means they last longer and adds a little bounce to make them print better.*

# Track shoes

*If you don't have access to a woodland or wild area, this is a lovely activity to get to know different animal tracks, without even having to leave your house! All you need to do is make the tracks yourself by creating giant animal-track flip-flops.*

**AGE** 5+ (with supervision)
**TIME** 1 hour
**TOOLS** Scissors, metal skewer, glue gun, paintbrush
**MATERIALS** Thick cardboard, foam sheets, paint, approx. 1yd (1m) of ¼in (6mm)-wide elastic (for two flip-flops), roll of paper

**Step 1**
Think about what kind of tracks you would like to make: deer, sheep, rabbit, dinosaur, whatever you like. Use an animal identification book to draw some accurate tracks and make your own templates out of cardboard. Or go to page 154 and trace or photocopy the ones we have provided.

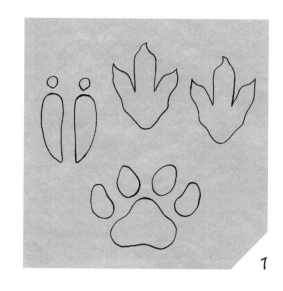
1

## Step 2

Draw the animal tracks on to thick cardboard (or trace/stick on your template). The only rule is that you can't draw a track longer than your own foot. Repeat to make a pair. You could even make two for the front legs and two for the hind legs!

## Step 3

Cut them out and glue them on to the foam sheet using the glue gun, then cut around them again. In order to make a clear print, you need to glue together a layer of cardboard and foam to create the depth the track needs to stand out.

## Step 4

Cut out two rectangles of card, about 1in (2.5cm) wider than your foot all around.

## Step 5

Place a bare foot on your cardboard rectangles. Now imagine you are wearing a flip-flop and put a cross where the flip-flop would sit between your big toe and the next toe. In the middle of your foot (where your foot arches), either side, draw another cross. This will be your guide when we turn the piece of card into a flip-flop.

## Step 6

Take your foot off the cardboard and, using your metal skewer, carefully make holes where the crosses are. Put extra layers of cardboard underneath where you are making the holes to protect your work surface underneath.

### Step 7
Cut about off about 6in (15cm) of elastic to make a toe loop. Find the centre of the elastic and fold it over so that the two ends meet. Thread the end with the loop through the hole you made next to the big toe, poking through about ¾in (2cm) through to the front of the flip-flop. Tie a knot on the back to secure it, making sure it doesn't slip through.

### Step 8
Using about 12in (30cm) of the elastic, tie a large knot (big enough so that it doesn't slip through the hole) in one end and thread the other end through from the back of one of the lower side holes, through the toe loop you just made and back through the other lower side hole. Tie a large knot on the back to secure (again, making it big enough so that it will not slip through). You should now have a cardboard flip-flop. Cut off any excess elastic and repeat for the other foot.

### Tip
*You can always add a squeeze of glue from the glue gun to your elastic, if needed.*

### Step 9
Glue your pre-prepared animal tracks on to the bottom of each flip-flop at the ball of your foot. Leave to dry until set.

### Step 10
Slip your flip-flops on and paint the tracks. You'll need to get a friend to help as you stand on one leg.

### Step 11
Walk across your paper to make a trail of animal footprints.

### More ideas
- You could make your tracks in secret and then get your friends to say which animal they think made the track.
- Do front and back tracks using both your hands and feet.
- Go fast, go slow, do both, and then get your friends to guess how the animal was moving.
- Using made-up tracks, decide with your friends what this animal could be like, based on its footprints.

# Nest challenge

*Have you ever found an old bird's nest? Did you have a really good look at it? Feel the weight of it, look at the intricate weave and all the materials inside? I've been lucky enough to find several and I have always been totally amazed. I love seeing the random, sometimes man-made, fibres used and wonder where they got them from. Tiny feathers get woven in, mud, grasses and sticks too – it's a creation of great beauty and strength. Could you create a nest yourself, just using your beak? OK, not your beak; try tweezers instead and you'll have some idea of the delicate task birds have!*

**AGE** 5+
**TIME** 10 minutes+
**TOOLS** Tweezers
**MATERIALS**
Foraged grasses, sticks, feathers (and anything else you can think of: be creative), a small plant pot, small branch/twig, some soil or rocks to hold the branch in place, chocolate mini eggs or marbles

### Step 1
Root your small branch or twig in your plant pot using either soil or stones to hold it in place. This is the tree that you will build your nest in.

### Step 2
Gather your nest-building materials together and pick them up, one at a time, using the tweezers. Balance each piece carefully on the chosen area of your tree. One by one, you will need to carefully place them and weave them together so that they hold firm.

### Step 3
When you think you have filled in enough gaps, try to balance your marbles or chocolate mini eggs in your nest and see if they stay safely in the nest.

**1**

**2**

## Variation
*Try using other tools as your beak – chopsticks or a peg, perhaps. Using small cut lengths of straw with suction to grab and drop sticks is a real challenge!*

### Birds' beaks
Did you know that birds' beaks are shaped according to their diet? Finches have a strong, cone-shaped beak (a bit like the tweezers), which they use to crack seeds with. Insect eaters, such as swallows, bluebirds and woodpeckers, have thin, pointed beaks (a bit like chopsticks), used to pick small insects off leaves. Hummingbirds have long beaks (like straws) that they use to suck nectar.

**3**

**AGE** 6+

**TIME** 1 hour

**TOOLS** Tray, bowl, sponge or spray bottles (optional but very useful), two rubber bands, darning needle, tea towel, scissors

**MATERIALS** Large piece of netting, approx. 30in (80cm) long and 10in (25cm) wide, 7oz (200g) merino wool tops in any colour you wish (available from craft suppliers), washing-up liquid (the bubblier the better), warm water, thick sewing thread, four 2yd (2m)-lengths of cotton fabric, 1½–2in (4–5cm) wide (two each of a different colour) for the handle.

# Felted nature bag

*Making your own bag out of felted wool is great for the planet and handy to use when out and about. Take it with you on your adventures, big or small, to collect the treasures you find. It's a simple, calm craft that we've found most children love losing themselves in.*

## Step 1

If you are using spray bottles, fill them with hot water from the tap and squeeze in two large squirts of washing-up liquid. If not, fill a large bowl with water as hot as your hands can cope with and add 2–3 large squirts of washing-up liquid.

## Step 2

Lay the netting out over the tray. There will be a large excess of netting hanging over the sides of the tray. You will be making a sheet of felted wool about 15 x 10in (40 x 25cm). Pull off long tufts of the wool and lay them vertically (bottom to top) on the netting, covering a 15 x 10in (40 x 25cm) area, overlapping each section by about ³⁄₈in (1cm).

1

**Tip**
*Merino wool tops are available from craft suppliers.*

2

## Step 3

Add more tufts of wool horizontally (left to right) over the first layer of wool, still overlapping each section. Repeat the criss-crossing of the wool until you have 3–4 layers.

## Step 4

Fold the overhanging netting over the wool and dampen it with the warm water. Either squirt water from the bottles or use the sponge dipped in the bowl of soapy water.

## Step 5

Gently press down on the wool to soak up the water, making sure it is wet all over.

## Step 6

Roll up the netting and wool carefully into a sausage shape, starting from the enclosed side, and add the rubber bands to the ends to hold them in place.

## Step 7

Lay the tea towel under your work area and use this to roll the whole piece back and forth while pressing. You can wrap the whole thing up in the tea towel as this allows you to grip better. Do this for about 10 minutes and add some more water and a squeeze of soap if needed.

## Tip

*Heat helps with felting so use hot (not boiling) water to speed up the process. If you have a tumble dryer, put in for 3–5 minutes – it will shrink so don't leave it for too long!*

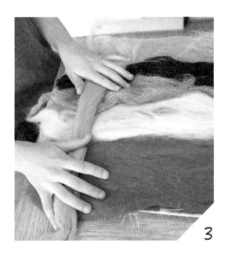

3

4

5

6

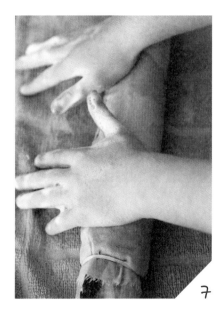

7

8

9

10

11

12

13

### Step 8

Undo the netting, gently peeling the wool away from the net.

### Step 9

You will know that the wool is successfully felted when the fibres are tightly packed together and firm. Run your fingers gently over the wool. If it all stays put, it's done. If the fibres still move around, roll back up and repeat the rolling process until it is done. Rinse with warm water and let dry.

### Step 10

When the felt is dry, trim the edges so it looks neat.

### Step 11

Now to make the bag shape. Fold the felted fabric almost in half but leave enough at the top for a flap.

### Tip

*If you want to make your fibres even tighter, you can ask an adult to help you use boiling water from the kettle. Put your piece of felt into the kitchen sink and gently, slowly, pour over hot water. This will help to shrink the wool so it is super tight. Wait until it is cool to squeeze it out.*

### Step 12

With the darning needle and thread, sew up the two sides of the bag. First, tie a knot in one end of the darning thread (you can also use knitting yarn to sew) and thread on to the needle. You will turn the bag inside out after the stitching is complete so think about which side of the felt you want to be on the outside.

### Step 13

Start from the bottom and use a running stitch, pushing the needle in and out, repeating until you get to the end of the folded section. Secure the end of the thread with a couple of stitches and cut the thread. Repeat on the other folded side and turn the bag right side out.

## Step 14

To make the handle, take the four long strands of cotton fabric and tie an overhand knot in one end (see page 17).

## Step 15

You will need help from two other friends with this next part. Stand opposite a friend who will be holding two strips of fabric, one in each hand, both in the same colour. You will hold the other two strips of another colour, one in each hand. Ask a third person to hold the knot, which is securing the strips together, up in the middle. Take the fabric strip in your left hand and swap it with your friend's strip in their left hand. Do the same with the material in your right hand. As you swap you will alternate colours. Keep going like this until you run out of fabric. Tie an overhand knot to secure the end.

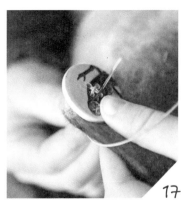

## Step 16

Attach the handle to your bag by sewing each end in place on the inside of the side seams at the top.

## Step 17

To hold down the flap, sew a button on to the front section of the bag. Using scissors, cut a buttonhole into the top flap by pinching the area where you want it to be and making a small cut. The felted fabric will not fray where you have cut it. Now all you need is a few essential items for an adventure, and you're off!

# Natural seed balls

**AGE** 3+
**TIME** 20 minutes
**TOOLS** Mixing bowl, measuring cup (could be a small cup from your kitchen or a small empty yoghurt pot)
**MATERIALS** Wildflower seeds (a native mix, if possible), water, peat-free compost, powdered clay (can be bought online) or air-dry clay

*Growing native wildflowers from these seed balls will help insects survive in built-up areas by giving them a vital food source. Attracting beasties to our homes and local area will benefit everyone and you can admire the amazing display at the same time. Try them in a plant pot on a balcony or front step.*

### Step 1
Mix together 1 cup of wildflower seeds with 4 cups of compost and 3 cups of powdered clay. To use air-dry clay instead, just pinch a golf-ball size piece of clay and break it into small pieces, mixing together the seeds and compost until they are completely combined.

### Step 2
Carefully and slowly, mix in a spoonful of water at a time until it all starts to hold together enough to be made into balls. If it gets too sloppy you can always add more compost.

### Step 3
Get your hands into the mixture and roll it into little balls. You can make them whatever size you like. The bigger they are the more seeds they will have in them.

### Step 4
Leave the balls to dry out overnight. If you want to wait before planting these, you can store them in an empty egg box in a cool, dark place. You can either throw your seed balls at bare patches of your garden or place them into pots.

1

*Tip*
*Butterflies and bees are attracted to different flowers. Butterflies like buddleja (buddleia), verbena, wild marjoram and pot marigolds. For bees, grow lavender, thyme, oregano, fennel, borage and foxgloves.*

2

3

4

# THINGS TO DO WITH CONKERS

*A favourite autumnal activity for many children is to go hunting for horse chestnuts (conkers) in the local park. The only problem is what to do with the large collection that accumulates at home. We've painted them, painted with them, drawn faces on them, used them in a bowl in a corner to fend off spiders, even made soap with them. Here are some of our favourite ideas.*

### Conker games

Draw a cross on some and a circle on others with acrylic paint pens. Make a criss-cross board with sticks and play tic-tac-toe (noughts and crosses).

### Conker facts

Conkers come from the horse chestnut tree *(Aesculus hippocastanum)* and are NOT edible. Horse chestnut trees have very large hand-shaped leaves, with 5–7 leaflets and spiky shells around the nut. Do not confuse with the sweet chestnut tree *(Castanea sativa)*, which has single long leaves and the chestnuts can be roasted and eaten.

### Conker soap

The seeds (conkers), the leaves and the bark of the horse chestnut tree all contain a very useful compound called saponin. Saponins have incredible cleaning properties and have been used for centuries for their similarities with soap. When your soapy mixture is ready, you can even put it in the washing machine as a biodegradable laundry soap or just use it to wash your hands. It should make suds, just like soap!

Grate the conkers into a bowl. You can also use a food processor to break them up but beware, this could make your blade blunt.

Pour warm water from the kettle to fill your glass jar. Add the grated conkers to the warm water. Leave it to steep. You can use the mixture after about half an hour, once it has turned milky, but it's even better left overnight.

Now all you need to do is use it to wash grubby hands, just like soap. Thoroughly rinse with warm water afterwards as conkers are toxic and must not be ingested.

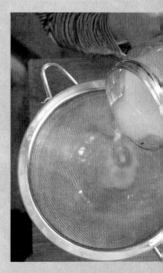

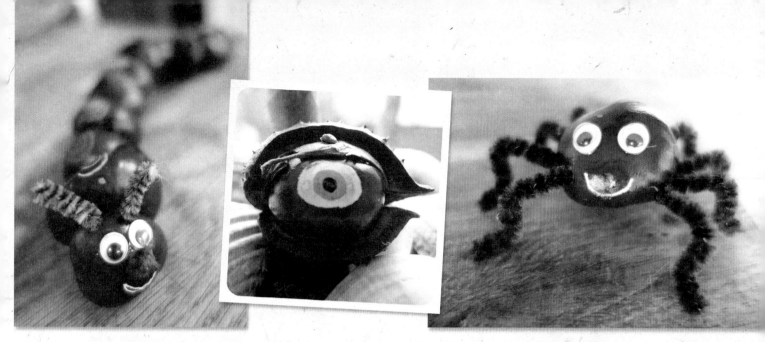

# Conker creations

### Conker streamers

Carefully make a hole in a conker using a screwdriver or metal skewer. Cut up long lengths of colourful tissue paper. Fill the hole in the conker with glue and then stuff the lengths of tissue paper into it, pressing firmly with the skewer or the end of a pencil. Wait to dry and then throw them in the air. They look lovely and make cool sounds too!

### Conker spiders

First make eight holes in the conker where you want the legs to be, using a screwdriver or metal skewer. Stick in pipe cleaners as legs. Glue on googly eyes.

### Conker people

Make a hole in the bottoms of two conkers using a screwdriver or metal skewer. Press one end of a cocktail stick into one conker and the other end into the hole in the other conker. They should now be attached together with some of the stick visible in the middle. Twist a pipe cleaner around this bit of visible stick to make the arms. Glue some wool on to the top

of one conker for hair, add some googly eyes and paint on a face with acrylic paint pens.

### Conker caterpillar

Using a screwdriver or metal skewer, make a hole all the way through each conker. About 10 is a good number. Using yarn and a blunt needle, thread through the conkers and tie a big knot at the end so that they don't fall off. Glue on googly eyes. Paint a design on the rest of the body.

### Conkers animals

Make holes as before for legs, ears, antlers etc. and press in whole or broken-up cocktail sticks. Try to break up lots of cocktail sticks and cover one whole side to make a cute little hedgehog.

### Conker art

To make homemade wrapping paper, all you need is a tray, some paper, paint and conkers. Lay the paper on the tray. Paint your conkers with thick paint and place on to the paper. Use the tray to roll the paint-covered conkers around to make colourful designs.

# Recipes

I LOVE COOKING AND I LOVE IT ESPECIALLY WHEN I GET
TO USE MY OWN FORAGED INGREDIENTS. I FIND THAT MY
SENSE OF SATISFACTION, KNOWING THAT I PICKED THE
INGREDIENTS, GIVES A MUCH MORE DELICIOUS TASTE,
WHATEVER I CHOOSE TO MAKE! BUT COOKING, PROCESSING
AND USING WILD PLANTS IS NOT ALL ABOUT MAKING
SOMETHING EDIBLE. SOMETIMES I LIKE TO MAKE BALMS
AND SALVES, USING NATURE'S SUPERPOWERS TO HEAL
MYSELF AND MY FRIENDS AND FAMILY.

# A guide to foraging

### Tip
*Make sure you pick above the level where dogs may relieve themselves and avoid areas where car fumes are high (roadside picking is not advisable).*

*Lots of yummy wild edibles grow in our cities and towns, not just in the countryside. Seeds can travel for miles on the wind and can often be found rooted along walls, grassy verges and roadsides. Our ancestors have been foraging for millions of years; it's in our blood to find wild greens, delicious edible berries and nuts, as well as the roots and the shoots of lots of useful plants. Luckily, these days we have reference books and experts that help us identify what to pick, and what to steer clear of. Even if you are looking for the most common, well-known plants, there are still lots of things to consider before you go out picking.*

Foraging can be great fun, as well as delicious, but always be mindful when out picking. Ask yourself these simple questions before you pick anything:

· Am I 100% sure that it is what I think it is?
· Do I need permission to pick here?
· Is there plenty for me to pick and still leave some to grow?
· Am I picking for a purpose?
· Is this a safe area to pick from?

## Plant identification
All the plants used in the recipes on the following pages can be found in the plant identification section on page 80. Remember, if you are not 100% positive, don't pick them.

If you are on private land you will need to ask permission from the landowner before you pick anything (yes, that does include asking a grown-up before you pick from the garden).

If the answer is not absolutely yes to every one of these questions, then re-think and don't pick.

Never assume that you know a plant. Have more than three identification features. Do not use smell alone as scent can transfer to your hands from another plant. REMEMBER: if you're not 100% sure, DO NOT PICK. You can either come back with a reference book later or bring someone who can definitively identify them for you.

If there are only one or two plants, consider leaving them to grow and be admired by other people as well as the wildlife who may rely on that plant. Do not clear a patch just for your own needs. Always leave enough to continue reproducing.

It's a good idea to have a plan. Once or twice I didn't do this, and the foraged plants ended up being wasted. It is better to choose a recipe before you go, so you know what you'll be using them for and how much you will need.

## Foraging tips
- Always try a little before you try a lot. Even when classed as edible, that doesn't always mean that your body will react in a positive way.
- Wear long trousers and long-sleeved tops to protect from brambles and nettles.
- Carry a small first-aid kit and a bottle of water.
- Take a small basket with you so as not to crush your delicious edibles in a bag.
- Make sure you go foraging with a responsible adult.
- As there are different laws when it comes to digging the roots of plants, leave these well alone for the time being, until you get expert advice on this subject.
- Just remember, IF IN DOUBT, LEAVE IT OUT!

# SOOTHING SALVES

*You can use many common herbs and plants to add a different healing property to a basic salve recipe. Below are some of my favourite plants that are readily available in towns and cities. Follow the infusing instructions for each plant and then use with the salve recipe. Semi-solid at room temperature, salves soften once applied to the skin, making them less messy than oils and absorbed easily into the skin.*

## Making an infused oil

Choose from the herbs and plants below and follow the drying instructions for each one. Put two cups of the dried plant material into a jar, cover completely with olive oil then cover the jar with a lid. Let the jar sit in a sunny place for two weeks; a windowsill inside is fine. Strain out the plant material using a muslin cloth and save the oil. Really squeeze the muslin cloth to get every bit of oil out.

### Daisy

Daisies are fantastic at helping to speed up the healing process for bruising and sprains. They are said to be anti-inflammatory and can help to reduce feelings of mild pain (but do not use on broken skin). Use two big handfuls of fresh daisy flower heads to make the infused oil.

### Plantain (broadleaf type)

Plantain is great for healing wounds, soothing burns, bringing down swelling and for treating bites or stings. Dry out the leaves first on a windowsill. Once dry and crinkly, grind in a food processor or break up by hand. Use two cups to make the infused oil.

### Dandelion

Use dandelion salve for sore muscles, achy joints and rough chapped skin. Pick the dandelions when they are fresh and in season. Dry out the flower heads for a day or two on a windowsill. Use two cups of dried flower heads to make the infused oil.

### Comfrey

Comfrey's original name, 'knitbone', derives from its medicinal properties that enable it to help heal burns, sprains, swelling and bruises when used externally. I love using comfrey salve to nourish dry skin on my hands as well as using it for aches and pains. Use only the leaves. Do not use on open wounds.

# Basic salve recipe (use your chosen plant-infused oil)

**AGE** 5+ (with supervision for the heating process)

**TIME** 20 minutes to make the salve with pre-prepared infused oil

**TOOLS** Bain-marie or double boiler (a glass bowl set in a saucepan), jug

**MATERIALS**
1 oz (25ml) beeswax (use carnauba wax for a vegan salve), 4 fl oz (100ml) herbal infused oil, lavender essential oil (optional),* clean glass or metal pots with lids to store it in, muslin cloth, vitamin E oil (optional, but can help to extend the salve's shelf life)

Makes 5 fl oz (125ml)

*\* Some essential oils are not recommended for use on the skin.*

## Tip
*Use clean jars, labelled correctly with what's inside, what it is to be used for and the date you made it.*

### Step 1
Measure your infused oil. Work out the proportions of oil and wax needed. For every four parts of oil, you need one part of beeswax. I had 4 fl oz (100ml) of oil and so I needed 1 oz (25ml) of beeswax.

### Step 2
In a bain-marie (or double boiler), combine the infused oil and beeswax. Heat gently and stir until completely melted.

### Step 3
Remove from the heat. Add approximately 10 drops of essential oil and 3–4 drops of vitamin E oil, if using. Allow to cool a little.

### Step 4
Transfer into a jug for ease of pouring, making sure your mixture has cooled a little but has not started to set. Pour into the clean pots and let them cool completely. Cover tightly and label. The salve should last for at least six months.

# Stinging nettle crisps

Nettles are, in my opinion, under-appreciated. Yes they can sting, but why not bite them before they bite you? They are delicious and so very good for you. Full of vitamins, calcium, potassium, iron and really high in protein, the best part is that they grow abundantly and are completely free.

**AGE** 5+ (with supervision)
**TIME** 10 minutes
**TOOLS** Washing-up gloves, tea towel, large bowl, baking sheet, oven

## Ingredients

**A bowlful of young nettle leaves**
**2 tbsp oil of your choice**
**1 tsp salt**
**1 tsp crushed red pepper flakes (optional)**
**1 tsp freshly ground pepper**
**2 tbsp nutritional yeast (optional but highly recommended, available at most supermarkets and health food shops)**

### Tip
*Crisps made from wild greens are best eaten on the day that they are made as they tend to lose their crunch over time. Now there's something you don't often get told, 'Eat them all up at once!'*

### Step 1
Be aware that until the nettles have been cooked, they will still have the ability to sting so wear washing-up gloves when preparing the leaves. Strip the leaves from the stems. Wash and dry them, patting them gently with a tea towel.

### Step 2
Combine all the seasoning ingredients and oil, including the nutritional yeast flakes if you are using them, in a large bowl and toss in the leaves, making sure they get a good coating.

### Step 3
Place the nettles on a baking sheet in a single layer. DO NOT be tempted to try one yet, otherwise you'll get an unpleasant reminder that until the leaves are cooked they will retain their sting!

### Step 4
Bake in a low oven at around 250°F (130°C) until they crisp up, turning once halfway through. This should be done in about 25 minutes. How long they take will depend on how much moisture there is in the leaves. When cool, place in a bowl and devour.

# Stinging nettle smoothie

I like this smoothie, a lot. I actually think it's rather delicious, but it's probably not for everyone. Our eternally honest eight-year-old daughter said, "I'm not really sure I liked the flavour, but I knew I could taste how good it was for me so I drank it all up anyway!" Give it a go. You might just like it!

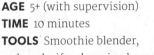

## Ingredients

- 1 banana
- ¼ pineapple
- 3 tbsp coconut milk
- ¼ cucumber (peeled and cubed)
- ½ avocado, for a creamier smoothie (optional)
- 1 handful stinging nettle leaves

## Step 1
You can either clean the nettles (see box, below) and use them immediately, or let them wilt overnight to reduce the sting factor while working with them.

## Step 2
Add all of the ingredients to the blender and mix really well. Make sure to blend long enough to end up with a smooth mixture. The nettles need to be shredded completely to ensure they will no longer sting.

**AGE** 5+ (with supervision)
**TIME** 10 minutes
**TOOLS** Smoothie blender, a glass, knife, chopping board, washing-up gloves for handling the nettles

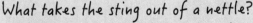

## What takes the sting out of a nettle?
- Cooking or pouring boiling-hot water over them.
- Crushing the needles.
- Letting them wilt over a couple of days.
- Dehydrating them and letting them dry to a crisp over a few weeks, or in a dehydrator.
- Blending them into a sauce/paste/smoothie.

# Garlic and butter nettles

Just like spinach, nettles taste great fried up in a pan with lashings of crushed garlic and a generous dollop of salted butter.

## Ingredients

3–4 handfuls of nettles
1 tbsp butter
1–2 cloves of crushed or sliced garlic
salt and pepper to season, if desired
grated cheese (optional)

### Step 1

Wearing gloves, chop up the nettles on a chopping board.

### Step 2

Heat a frying pan and fry the nettles with the butter and garlic until they are wilted (about five minutes). Add a little salt to taste and enjoy with a poached egg on toast, or use them on top of pizza or pasta for a hint of brilliant green. You could also add grated cheese at the end.

## Picking and cleaning stinging nettles

See page 134 to make sure that you know what you are picking. To avoid getting stung, wear long-sleeved tops and trousers when harvesting, and gloves. You can use scissors and cut directly into a bowl to avoid having to handle them at all. Pick the first two or three pairs of leaves from the tops of the plants as these will be the most tender. Carefully place the nettles into a bag or container for transporting.

Clean the nettles by swishing them around (wearing gloves) in a large sink or basin filled with cool water. Lift the nettles out, leaving any grit behind, and drain them.

# Barbecue bannock bread

This simple, flat, baked dough is quick and easy to make and delicious to eat. Some parks allow you to bring along a disposable barbecue and light it and some do not. If you are unsure, phone or contact your local council. They should be able to let you know the details. Some parks even provide a special barbecue area. If you can't use your local park, try another outdoor area, garden or even a front yard.

## Ingredients

**Flour, pinch of salt, bottle of water, resealable bag (you can add anything extra to your basic mix: herbs, cheese, chilli, cinnamon, raisins, sugar, etc.)**

**AGE** 6+ (with adult supervision)
**TIME** 30 minutes
**TOOLS** Pair of tongs, a disposable barbecue, or you can even use a fire-pit area if you have access to one in your garden.

## Tip
*Flames are for boiling, coals are for cooking.*

### Step 1
Light the disposable barbecue. You need the hot coals to cook on, not the flames, so light it in advance so that the fire can die down to lovely hot embers.

### Step 2
Mix up the dry ingredients in a resealable bag. One small handful of flour is about enough for a single portion. You can add grated cheese and dried herbs for a savoury bread or you might prefer a sweet version with cinnamon and sugar.

### Step 3
Pour water, a few drops at a time, into the resealable bag and gently squish around until thoroughly combined. It should resemble the consistency of playdough. Keep adding water until you achieve the perfect dough. If it gets too wet, just add more flour.

### Step 4
Roll out small balls of dough (about the size of a satsuma) in your hands and gently squish to make small, flat patties.

### Step 5
When your coals are ready, place the dough patties straight on to the coals and cook for a minute or two on each side, turning with a pair of tongs. When they are ready, take them off the fire and leave them to cool.

142

# Garlic mustard pesto sauce

This plant is one of my favourites. It's easy to identify by the little clusters of white flowers, distinct smell and the nettle-like look of its leaves. Check in our identification section on page 81 to find out all about this plant, how to harvest it and what it looks like.

## Ingredients

2 cups garlic mustard leaves
¼ cup extra virgin olive oil
¼ cup grated Parmesan cheese
¼ tsp sea salt
2 tsp apple cider vinegar
1 tsp balsamic vinegar
2 garlic cloves
¼ cup pine nuts or almonds
1 tbsp mayonnaise and 1 tbsp
  of Greek yoghurt (optional)

## Step 1

Whether you are making a dip or a pesto, prepare by putting all of the ingredients in a blender and whizz together until a paste is formed (add water to make a looser sauce for stirring through pasta).

## Step 2

Season to taste. Either mix through pasta, use as a pizza base sauce or add 1 tbsp of mayonnaise and 1 tbsp of Greek yoghurt to use it as a dip.

**AGE** Any (supervision with foraging)
**TIME** 10 minutes
**TOOLS** Blender

## Tip

*Remember, do not pick anything unless you are 100% sure you can identify it.*

## Garlic mustard salad

These potent little leaves are pretty tasty as they are. Pick a handful and add to a bowl of spinach and rocket leaves. Drizzle with olive oil, the juice of one lemon and add salt and pepper. Toast some pumpkin and sunflower seeds and scatter over the top. Hey presto, a delicious salad!

# Dandelion cookies

Dandelions are overlooked as weeds by so many people, but I know that they are magical little plants. Haven't we all made wishes by blowing their fluffy little seed heads? OK, so they may not technically be magical, but they are incredible little things, packed full of vitamins and nutrients and completely edible. Their sunshine-coloured petals have a faint honey-like flavour, which is why I like to add them to cookies.

**AGE** 3+ (with supervision to put in the oven)
**TIME** 30 minutes
**TOOLS** Baking sheet and/or silicone baking mat, sieve, mixing bowl, spoon

## Tip
*Dandelions are best picked during the autumn or spring when they are more tender and less bitter.*

## Ingredients

½ cup butter, softened
½ cup 100% peanut butter
½ cup honey
1 egg
1 tsp vanilla extract

1 tsp baking powder
1 cup plain flour
1 cup wholewheat flour
½ cup dandelion petals

## Preparing the dandelions

Snip the dandelion petals from the flower. It's OK to get a few bits of green in the cookies, but mostly you'll want the yellow petals for optimum flavour. Too much green stuff, and the cookies might take on an unpleasant bitter taste. It does take a little time, but it is worth it.

### Step 1
Preheat the oven to 350°F (180°C). Line a baking sheet with greaseproof paper or a silicone baking mat.

### Step 2
Sift together the flours and baking powder and set aside.

### Step 3
Cream together the butter, peanut butter and honey until light and fluffy. Beat in the egg and vanilla extract until thoroughly incorporated.

### Step 4
Add the sifted dry ingredients to the butter mixture and mix until a soft dough forms. Gently fold in the dandelion petals.

### Step 5
Drop spoonfuls on to your prepared baking sheet. Bake in the preheated oven for about 15 minutes, or until the edges are golden. Cool on a wire rack.

# Dandelion honey

This recipe couldn't be more simple and has lots of medicinal properties. It can be taken by the teaspoon for sore throats, as an energy booster, stirred through tea or added to the juice of a lemon and drunk as a remedy for a cold, or even spread on toast!

**AGE** Any
**TIME** 5 minutes
**TOOLS** Small glass jar, knife

### Note
Dandelion is safe for most people but is not recommended if you have active gallstones or are on a prescription diuretic.

### Ingredients
**1 handful of fresh dandelion petals**
**Jar of good-quality honey**

### Step 1
Prepare the dandelion petals as described on page 144 and stuff them into a small jar. Slowly pour the honey over them and fill the jar to the top. Stir with a knife to remove any air bubbles and put the lid on.

### Step 2
Let the jar sit in a cupboard for several days to allow the flowers to infuse into the honey.

### Step 3
Leave the flowers in and spoon around them. You can actually eat the honeyed flowers by the spoonful too. I find them to be quite delicious!

# Dinner at the allotment

*By Rachel Walmsley*

SOMETIMES IT'S THE SIMPLE THINGS THAT INDELIBLY MARK OUR MEMORIES AND ALTHOUGH MY CHILDHOOD WAS PEPPERED WITH THEATRE TRIPS, BIRTHDAY PARTIES AND THE OCCASIONAL SAFARI PARK, IT'S NOT THOSE EXPERIENCES THAT MAKE ME SMILE WHEN I RECALL THEM. IT'S THE SPONTANEOUS ONES THAT ARE MOST PRECIOUS AND REMIND ME THAT SOMETIMES THE THINGS THAT COST THE LEAST ARE ACTUALLY THE MOST VALUABLE.

As a child I loved summer evenings. The way the light seemed to stretch out, the way rules seemed to relax or not apply at all and the way that my body seemed to have endless energy for running about. My sisters and I were always outside, finding ways to make our parents forget we existed in order to delay bedtime. It was a summer filled with these types of evenings when our parents decided it was time to have an allotment, a small patch of land rented to people to be able to grow their own food. A precious 'wild' space, particularly for those living in towns and cities.

> *"The allotment had to become an adventure, and so they created one for us."*

Small children and vegetable planting seemed like the perfect combination, but in reality, three siblings all under the age of 10 trying to rake and dig in a tiny plot alongside their parents apparently was not going to lead to ripe tomatoes and abundant green beans but more to injury and squabbles. For a good few weeks, our parents convinced themselves they could create the harvest of fresh vegetables they'd always dreamed of while living in a town house with a small, dark garden. However, having taken the project on so late in the season they were disappointed by their progress. Busy with their jobs and three young children to look after, it was a challenge for them to find time to simply weed the overgrown plot, let alone plant a hopeful row of seedlings.

I recall the evening they decided that the allotment was no longer a separate 'extra job' for one of them to do once the children were in bed, but instead something all of us could be part of. There may have been an epiphany, a lightbulb moment or perhaps just a simple realization that the allotment needed to become an integral part of our life as a family. The allotment had to become an adventure, and so they created one for us.

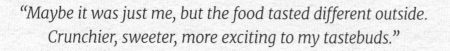

*"Maybe it was just me, but the food tasted different outside.
Crunchier, sweeter, more exciting to my tastebuds."*

I remember the quick change out of school uniforms and arriving at the allotment just as the sun spread that golden summer light over the town. Out of a cardboard box they pulled cold roast chicken, hard-boiled eggs, a rustic potato salad, some lettuce leaves and camping knives and forks. We upturned the cardboard box and perched on wooden crates around our makeshift table. Maybe it was just me, but the food tasted different outside. Crunchier, sweeter, more exciting to my tastebuds. And my sisters did agree! We felt like rule breakers – dinner outside, early evening sunshine on our faces, plastic cutlery and no parental supervision (they were finally happily busy digging and planting).

For the next few weeks our dinner picnics at the allotment were a regular occurrence and something we all remember with great fondness. It's hard to say if we actually did any gardening during this time; we may have done some 'helpful' weeding or watering, or maybe we just pottered around searching for broken pottery and nice rocks, but we were probably just too full of roast chicken to get into too much misadventure by this point.

# Blackberry chutney

We all know that these delicious berries are super sweet and make a great pudding, but what if I told you they also go brilliantly with cheese and curries? Sounds good? Sounds yucky? Give this chutney a go, then make up your mind — you might just be surprised.

### Ingredients
18 oz (500g) blackberries
5 oz (140g) caster sugar
5 oz (140g) red onions, sliced
3 tbsp chopped fresh root ginger
2 tbsp Dijon mustard
5¼ fl oz (150ml) white wine vinegar
salt and pepper

Makes about 14 fl oz (400ml)

**AGE** 6+ (with supervision when cooking on the stove)
**TIME** 30–40 minutes
**TOOLS** Saucepan, large spoon, heatproof jug, ladle, four 3½ fl oz (100ml) sterilized jars (see below)

### Sterilizing jars
You can reuse old jam jars and sterilize them, with adult supervision. Wash the jars and the lids in hot soapy water, but do not dry them. Instead, leave them to stand upside down on a roasting tray while they are still wet. Pop the tray of clean, wet jars and lids into a preheated oven at 325–350°F (160–180°C) for about 15 minutes.

### Step 1
Combine all the ingredients, except the vinegar, in a large saucepan.

### Step 2
Stir the mixture over a medium heat until you can see that all the blackberries have burst.

### Step 3
Add the vinegar and allow the mixture to simmer uncovered for 10 mins.

### Step 4
Season with salt and pepper, to taste. Leave to cool a bit (about 15 minutes or so will be fine) so that when ladling it into the jars it's not scalding hot if you touch it by accident.

### Step 5
Transfer the mixture into sterilized jars (see box, left) by ladling the hot mixture into a heatproof jug and pouring it into the jars. Be very careful not to get any of the mixture on to the rim of the jars as this could introduce bacteria. Fill the jars not quite to the top, leaving about a ¼in (½cm) gap at the top. While everything is still hot, cover the jars with their lids and seal immediately. If you don't have jar lids you can use wax paper or plastic wrap secured with an elastic band.

### Step 6
Once stored in sterilized jars, your chutney should keep for about six months in a cool, dark place and in the fridge, once opened. Serve with cheese and crackers or a lovely curry, perhaps.

# Spiced blackberry sorbet

I love picking blackberries until my fingers are stained purple and my tongue fizzes with delightful sweetness. But sometimes I would like to make the eating experience last longer than a passing delve into a thorny bush. So I tried this recipe and wasn't disappointed. The only trouble is having the willpower to get enough blackberries home to make it!

## Ingredients
4 cups (560g) blackberries
2½ cups (600ml) water
2 tbsp (30ml) lemon juice
½–1 cup (100–200g) coconut sugar or cane sugar (you can experiment with other sweeteners too: honey, maple syrup, date syrup etc.)

## Step 1
Rinse the blackberries, then combine in a blender with the water and lemon juice. Whizz until smooth, then press the mixture through a sieve and discard the seeds.

## Step 2
Place the blackberry mixture and sugar in a saucepan. Bring to the boil and reduce to a simmer. Let it cook for 1–2 minutes, until the sugar is fully dissolved.

## Step 3
Remove from the heat, transfer into a container and place it in the refrigerator to chill completely.

## Step 4
Once it has cooled down, pour the mixture into a shallow pan and place in a freezer for approximately 1 hour, or until frozen solid. Once frozen, break it into pieces and whizz in a blender or food processor until creamy and freeze again for 20 minutes. This process breaks up the ice crystals to give a smoother sorbet.

**AGE** Any (with supervision when cooking the blackberries)
**TIME** 1½ hours
**TOOLS** Blender, sieve, saucepan, shallow pan

## Variation
Try adding some herbs or spices, ginger perhaps (fresh or dried) or maybe some mint leaves, during the boiling process. Give it a go. Let your taste buds guide you.

# Blackberry and apple crumble

It's simple, it's delicious and it includes three of your five a day, so it must be healthy, right? Well, healthy-ish anyway.

**AGE** 3+ (with supervision)
**TIME** 45 minutes
**TOOLS** Apple corer (or sharp knife and spoon), two mixing bowls, aluminium foil, deep baking tray or roasting tin, sharp knife, fork or lemon squeezer, cup

## Ingredients

4 apples
8½ oz (250g) blackberries
2 tbsp honey or 1 tbsp brown sugar
1 tsp cinnamon (optional)

For the topping:
1 oz (30g) plain flour
2½ oz (75g) butter, softened
½ oz (15g) oats
½ oz (15g) demerara sugar
1 orange
¼ cup water

## Tip
*If you have a bird feeder, why not put the apple cores out for the birds? If not, just put them in the compost.*

## Step 1
Preheat the oven to 350°F (180°C, fan 160°C, gas mark 4). De-core the apples. You can either use an apple corer or a knife to carefully cut around the top of the core and dig it out with a metal spoon. Whichever method you use, scoop out around the core area with the spoon to create a wider cavity.

## Step 2
Using a sharp knife, make a slit in the skin the whole way around the apple. It will stop them from bursting. Do not cut all the way through!

## Step 3
In a mixing bowl, mix the blackberries, honey or sugar and cinnamon, if you're using, until all the berries are coated.

## Step 4
Place the apples into the baking dish and fill the holes with the blackberry mixture.

## Step 5
Blend the flour and butter in a mixing bowl using your fingers, rubbing the flour into the butter until the mixture looks like breadcrumbs. Now stir in the oats and the brown sugar and sprinkle over each apple.

## Step 6
Juice the orange using a fork or juice squeezer, being careful not to get any pips in, and combine it with the water. Pour this mixture into the bottom of the baking tray or roasting dish.

## Step 7
Cover with foil and bake for 20 minutes, or until the apples are soft. Remove the foil and put it back in the oven for a final 10 minutes so that the top can crisp up.

## Step 8
Serve warm with ice-cream (try the blackberry sorbet recipe on page 149), cream, Greek yoghurt or custard.

## Tip
*Don't forget to wipe the foil clean so that you can reuse it.*

# Track templates

*Photocopy at 100% and use with the Track shoes activity on page 120.*

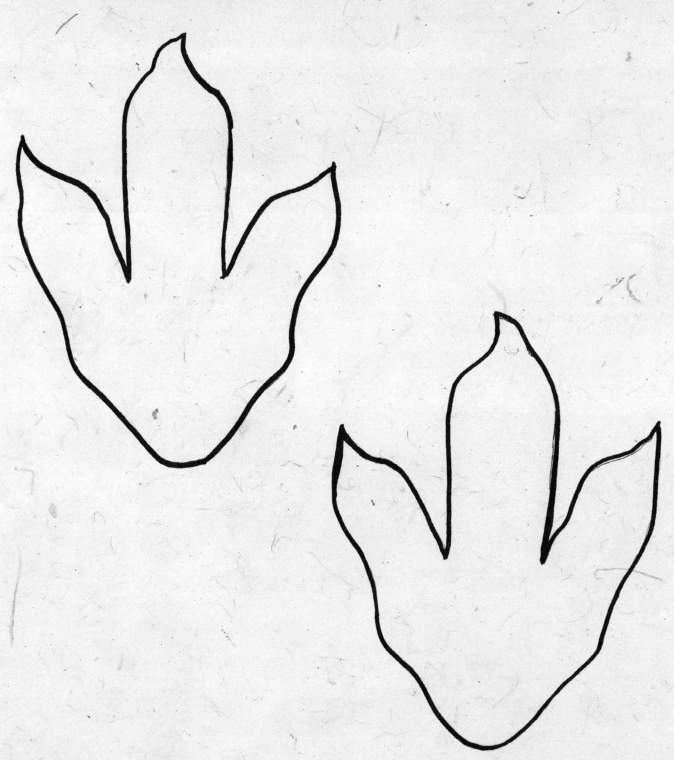

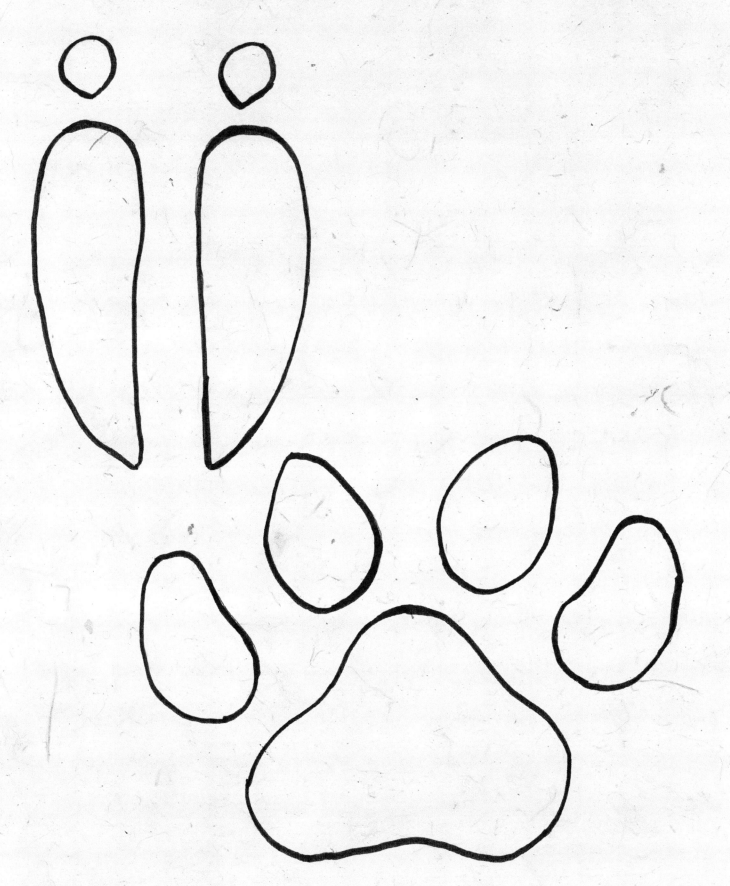

# Resources

## Books

*Little Book for Big Changes*
by Karen Ng and Kirsten Liepmann,
Studio Press, 2018

*Wild in the City*
Lonely Planet Kids, 2019

*The Wild City Book*
by Jo Schofield and Fiona Danks,
Frances Lincoln, 2014

*Anywhere Farm*
by Phyllis Root,
Walker Books, 2017

## Websites

www.forestschoolassociation.org
www.outback2basics.co.uk

# About the authors

Dan Westall and Naomi Walmsley run Outback2Basics from their patch of woodland in Shropshire, UK. Specializing in bushcraft and Stone Age skills, they provide unique experiences for schoolchildren and teachers to connect to nature. Dan has been a bushcraft teacher for many years and has also acted as a medic and survival consultant on various TV shows. Naomi is a qualified bushcraft instructor and Forest School Leader and believes that every child should be able to safely light a fire and have at least ten uses for a stick by the age of ten. She has also written about bushcraft and parenting for many magazines, including *Bushcraft & Survival Skills*, *Living Woods* and *Juno*. Together, they undertook a five-month Stone Age immersion experience in the US, living in the wilderness without any modern equipment, profoundly influencing their lives and teaching. They have recently taken part in a similar experience in Bulgaria, which was filmed for Channel 4 in the UK. Their previous book for GMC Publications is *Forest School Adventure*.

www.outback2basics.co.uk

# Acknowledgements

We would like to thank all the parents that gave up their children for us to photograph, no matter what the weather was, packing picnics and extra enthusiasm! We'd like to thank all the amazing children that gave up their free time to be directed around by us. You were all such brilliant models: patient, happy and willing! I'd also like to thank our daughter Maggie for all her help with the book, trying out activities and being a brilliant, constantly on-hand model. Even when she really did not want to be in any more photos, she always did one more, just for me. And thank you to Nick Lee and Christian Rwirangira for taking such wonderful photos.

## Picture credits

All photos by Dan Westall, Nick Lee (reflectivenature. co.uk) and Christian Rwirangira except the following from Shutterstock.com:

Pages 1, 2, 5 top right, centre, 6, 7 top left, centre and bottom, 8 except top cemtre, 9, 10, 12 top left, middle, 14, 33 bottom, 61, 63, 64 top right, 65, 66, 67, 68, 69, 74, 75, 76, 77, 78, 79 except right centre (top), 80, 81, 82, 83, 87 except right centre (bottom), 91, 92, 93, 111 except right, 116, 117, 129 bottom (both), 130 left, 133, 134, 135, 136 except bottom (left), 140 centre, 143, 144 left, 145, 148, 150 left, 152, 160.

Illustration on inside covers by Rebecca Mothersole/GMC.

First published 2020 by
Guild of Master Craftsman Publications Ltd, Castle Place, 166 High Street, Lewes, East Sussex BN7 1XU, UK

Reprinted 2021

Text © Dan Westall and Naomi Walmsley, 2020. Copyright in the Work © GMC Publications Ltd, 2020

ISBN 978 1 78494 563 3

A catalogue record for this book is available from the British Library.

*Publisher* Jonathan Bailey

*Production Manager* Jim Bulley

*Senior Project Editor* Virginia Brehaut

*Managing Art Editor* Gilda Pacitti

*Illustrator* Sarah Skeate

*Colour origination* GMC Reprographics

Printed and bound in China

# Index

**A**

allotments 8, 146–147
ants 75
apples 27, 28, 150–151

**B**

badgers 61, 68, 91–92, 93
bags 13, 124–127
bannock bread 142
barbecues 142
bark rubbings 26
bats 91
bees 32, 75, 129
beeswax wraps 106–107
benefits of outdoor play 10–11
bird feeders 27–30, 50–51
birds 69, 79, 92, 93, 123
birds' nests 123
blackberries 83, 148–151
  chutney 148
  crumble 150
  sorbet 149
board games 56–57
botanical interactive art 34–35
bowling 42
bread 142
broadleaf plantain 83, 136
bubbles 36–39
bugs 74–75, 79
bunting 112–113

**C**

camping 48–49, 85
cats 61, 67, 91
cemeteries 9
chutney 148
climate change 14–15
cloud spotting 64–65
clove hitch 16
colour chart nature matching 88
comfrey 136
conkers 130–131
cookies 144
crisps 138

**D**

daisies 80, 136
dandelions 80, 136
  cookies 144
  honey 145
dangers 11, 91, 134, 135
dawn 67, 69, 91, 92
deer 92, 103
dens 52–55
dusk 67, 69, 91, 92, 93

**E**

earth worms 75
easel trees 26
eating outside 142, 147
eco-leaf printing 98–99
electricity, saving 15
English oak trees 79
equipment 13, 91, 124–125

**F**

fat balls 30
felting 96–97, 124–127
flowers 80–81, 136, 144, 145
food, growing 15, 48, 114–117
foraging 134–135
foxes 61, 67, 91

**G**

games 42–43, 56–57
gardens 24–25, 48–49
garlic 140
garlic mustard 80
  pesto sauce 143
  salad 143
grass snakes 72–73
growing food 15, 48, 114–117

**H**

hedgehogs 61, 68–69, 90
herbs 114–115
honey 144
honey bees 32, 75, 129
horse chestnut trees 79

**I**

insect water stations 32
interactive art 34–35

**J**

journals 13, 108–111

**K**

kites 12
kits 13, 91, 124–127
knots 16–19

**L**

ladybirds 74
leaf bunting 112–113
leaf identification 76, 77, 78
leaf printing 98–99, 100–101
lime trees 79
locations 8–9, 48–49
London plane trees 77

**M**

measuring sticks 13, 104
moles 61
moon 8, 92
mud, playing with 46–47

**N**

nature
  respecting 11
  where to look 8–9, 48–49
nature weaving 40–41
nest challenge 123
nettles 82, 138–140
nightime walks 90–91

**O**

oak trees 79
outdoor play, importance of 10–11
outdoor theatres 22–23
overhand knot 17
owls 92

## P

painting  12, 26, 44–45
parks  8
pencils  13
peripheral vision  70, 71
pesto sauce  143
picnics  147
pigeons  61, 69
pine-cone deer  103
places to look  8–9, 48–49
planning  11, 13
plantain  83, 136
planting food  15, 48, 114–117
plants  80–83, 114–117, 134–136
plastic, avoiding  15, 96, 106
potatoes  117
printing  98–99, 100–101

## R

rain painting  12
rats  61
recipes  136–151
recycling  15
rivers  84, 85
road safety  11
rowan trees  77

## S

safety  11, 91, 134, 135
salads  143
salves  136–137
scavenger hunts  86–87
seed balls  128–129
senses, using  70, 71
shadow painting  44–45
shear lashing  17
sheet bend  18
sheet dens  52–55
shelters  52–55
silver birch trees  76
sit spots  70–71
skies  8, 92
slip knot  18
smoothies  139

snail races  33
snakes  72–73
snakes and ladders  57
soap  96–97, 130–131
sorbet  149
squirrels  61, 66
stars  92
stick boats  118–119
stinging nettles  82
  crisps  138
  garlic and butter nettles  140
  smoothie  139
strawberries  117
string  13
suburbs  84–85

## T

tents  52–55
theatres, outdoor  22–23
tic-tac-toe  56, 57
timber hitch  19
toy swaps  15
track identification  61
track shoes  120–122, 154–155
track traps  58–61
treasure hunts  86–87
trees  76–79

## W

walking  11, 15, 90–91
water stations  32
watercolour printing  100–101
weather conditions  12
weaving  40–41
where to look  8–9, 48–49
wildflower seed balls  128–129
wildflowers  80–83, 128–129
wildlife spotting  61, 66–67, 90–93
willow hanging ball  50–51
wind  12
worms  75

To order a book, contact:
GMC Publications Ltd, Castle Place,
166 High Street, Lewes, East Sussex,
BN7 1XU, United Kingdom
Tel: +44 (0)1273 488005
www.gmcbooks.com